# The Last Dance

## A Memoir of the Garden Island Grille

### DAVE TRENTLAGE

Softcover ISBN: 978-1-66787-787-7
eBook ISBN: 978-1-66787-788-4

This book is dedicated to the memory of Robert Kanahele

His strength of character and guiding
hand allowed us to reach our dream

A great Hawaiian

A great chef

A great friend

He left behind so much to be proud of

Rest in peace kanaka

# CONTENTS

# The gathering storm

As I sat on the terrace of the Grand Hyatt resort in Poipu, Kauai, watching the day fade away into another magnificent sunset, I could not have imagined what was approaching out of the gathering darkness. It was a thing of indescribable proportions, moving with purpose, as it slowly and methodically made its way toward us. The date was March 10, 2020, and I was taking up space at a small table in the open air. It was a day that I will never forget. I was sipping on a cocktail with a view of the ocean in front of me and a scented breeze tugging at my shirt, settled comfortably in a plush chair at one of the finest resorts on the island. Unknown to me then, it was also the last time that I was truly optimistic about the direction of our future. That day, for me at least, marked the end of an era, not just in my life, but for the entire world.

My wife and I owned a restaurant in a small town not far from where we were sitting, and after five years of struggle and sacrifice, we had made it to a place we could be proud of. This was an opportunity for us to enjoy a drink with friends and take a little pleasure in how far we had come. I was calm, relaxed, and very excited about the direction our life was taking. My thoughts were so filled with the dream that we had turned into reality, and the future that appeared so bright, that I could not see the danger lurking around the corner. Our restaurant on that tiny island was the center of our entire world, the axis that our life on Kauai revolved around.

Sheri was sitting next to me stirring her drink and, no doubt lost in the same thoughts that I was having. Several years ago, we left our secure but unsettled lives in Michigan to chase our desires. I spent most of my life drowning in a career that I had no real interest in. When I met Sheri she was in the same boat, muddling through a job that was just that, a job. No room to express yourself. No avenues in this stern business world to put passion on display, or seek the hidden images that forever teased and hinted at a life where the things that really moved us could be set free.

Separately, we were stuck in a continuous circle of making ends meet, trudging off daily to a place that was at best a means to retirement, a steady path to an unfulfilled life. Together, however, we cultivated ideas of what a future based on what we actually wanted would look like.

My long-held desire to someday live in the tropics and open a tiki bar that served the world was a dream that I carried locked inside my head, knowing full well that I didn't possess the courage required to pursue it alone. Working for my father was something I knew was inevitable from a young age and while circumstances led me to that place, it was my lack of self-belief that kept me there. Sheri changed that and together we made a leap that, for most, crossed the boundaries of reasonable thinking.

Through it all, we chased that dream to where it led and, in the process, brought to light everything our hearts had ever hoped for. We had found success in a business where the odds are highly in favor of failure. The restaurant we created and the reputation we built was a struggle that went beyond anything we ever experienced before, but our single-minded dedication had lifted The Garden Island Grille above the masses and placed us every year in the top ten of all the restaurants on that beautiful island.

In the beginning, we met a few people claiming to be restauranteurs on Kauai, giving us their advice on everything from staffing to keeping the beer cold, and telling us that they have all the answers to success in that ever-shifting industry, only to see them close up shop and disappear within the first year. So often those failures came from not grasping what side of the bar they belonged on.

One, in particular, invited us as his guests to see the model he was creating and to watch how someone in the business gets it done. His words, not mine. When we arrived and found him at the bar, he was so drunk that he couldn't articulate his words let alone teach us anything he might have known. We knew then that to survive and succeed we needed to let our common-sense guide us.

Today was not a day of reflection, however, but a time to look ahead. Two of our closest friends were set to join us, so this was an unhurried moment to sit down with people we trusted and discuss the future of our restaurant. We were in the midst of our biggest tourist season to date and our minds were filled with images of what the coming years would bring. Everything pointed up.

The lease at our current location would be renewed in the next few weeks and we were laying our plans for the road ahead. A couple of places now wanted us as tenants, options we didn't have when we first opened. But we were happy with the location we were in. We had a reasonable lease arrangement, no debt, and the restaurant was successful enough to allow us a good living in Hawaii. We had achieved something most people only dream about.

The idea that a pandemic was crouching at our doorstep was something that never crossed our minds. Why would it? For all the planning we had done concerning the future of the Garden Island Grille, not once did we ever anticipate a virus that would shut down the world. We were moving forward as we always had, looking ahead every year at what would give us the best chance to succeed. There was no prior knowledge or precedence to even consider the thought. Among all the hazards that my insurance guy listed, this was not one of them.

It's so puzzling to look back and remember that day, sitting there at the Hyatt. Everything around us was exactly what you'd expect if you were gathered around a table at a lavish resort in sun-drenched Hawaii. Couples holding hands wandered the shops that lined the open lobby, families huddled together in animated conversation, and a trio of musicians were tuning their instruments for happy hour. I could see the bartenders were busy rattling ice in their shakers and pouring out fun and festive tropical drinks. Hawaiian print dresses and aloha shirts swirled through the open space in every color and tropical pattern imaginable.

The gentle breeze was perfumed with the aroma of hibiscus, as it softly stirred around us. We were overlooking the unbounded Pacific Ocean, sparkling like a jewel in the late afternoon sun. Off to the left, I could just make out a sliver of white sand as it slipped around Shipwreck Bay. It was perfect. I didn't know then that it would turn out to be one of the last normal days we've had since. Even with the power of hindsight, we couldn't have seen that we stood in the crosshairs of a raging tempest.

Covid-19 was in the news and gaining strength, but to this point, we had no real idea what it was, or what it would ultimately mean. People on the island talked about it in terms of what-ifs, and here's what I heard, but it wasn't a topic that filled long discussions. It's hard to believe that we were more concerned with our upcoming lease renewal. Kauai seemed so far removed that the fears over the outbreak that was sweeping the mainland simply hadn't arrived on our shores.

When Brock and Eve finally arrived and joined us, we took a minute to sit back and enjoy the view. This was a rare moment away from work and we were in no rush to let it pass by. Our talk centered around the restaurant, but other things were sprinkled in as well. Not once did the conversation drift in the direction of Covid, or anything relating to it. We were isolated on an island in the middle of nowhere. It's not that we didn't care, or that we were burying our heads, it just wasn't on our radar.

When we moved from Michigan to Kauai and started the Garden Island Grille, we did so without any prior restaurant or food handling experience. We were two people making a living who wanted something else out of life. I had worked in the plumbing business for so long that it had simply run out of challenges and became more of a means to an end rather than a love for the job, which I never really had anyway.

We re-learned and re-invented the rest of our lives and followed that dream to Kauai. Without any support on the island, we were miraculously handed an opportunity that we poured our hearts and minds into. In the process, through a lot of hard work and absolute determination, we were able to conquer every obstacle that fell in our path. Until this.

This is a story that for me seems improbable, especially considering the background I came from, yet I lived it. As I sit here now, relating this surprising tale, I never would have predicted then that twilight had fallen. That our bamboo stage that provided a platform for so many musicians would be dark and silent, or that the energy and excitement that made The Garden Island Grille what it was, a place to come together, would be stilled. I could not have imagined that within a week our dream would come crashing down and the restaurant that we put our hearts into would close its doors forever.

## CHAPTER 1

# The story begins with Randy

Alone figure moved silently along the deserted lane. The narrow access ran behind the shops and restaurants that make up the epicenter of the small town of Koloa. Like a shadow, he clung to a row of trees and tall bushes as he traversed the opposite side of the road as if to go unnoticed in his journey. Just a dark silhouette slowly passing through the strange glow of a fading rain. As he came closer the light shifted and danced with the scudding clouds, and his features began to take shape. The ragged hem of a dark, oil-skin duster, flapping around unhurried ankles. A screen of long, black hair, lying about his neck like a limp curtain. A bulky pack shrugged over one shoulder, and a head that never shifted from the ground at his feet.

I was out there to escape the drawn and troubled faces of not just my employees, but almost everyone I was running into. I drifted aimlessly around the back door of the restaurant, wearing a circle in the tiny expanse of lawn that covered the septic tank, which was ironic since everything seemed to be turning to shit. It was a measure of peace, and hopefully a little quiet that I was seeking, an evasion of the questions for which I had no answers, from the people who needed them the most. My employees were looking to me for guidance and reassurance, and while I could offer them platitudes, I had nothing in the way of answers, because I was as much in the dark as they were. The news and events of the past week since I sat at the Hyatt, oblivious to what was coming, had all conspired to derail a dream and shake the very foundation of our future.

A rainbow, nothing more than an everyday occurrence here on Kauai, was a good enough excuse to drop what I was doing and get some fresh air. As aimless as it felt at times, my entire life had led me to where I am now. I had finally reached a place where I knew who I was, and what I wanted. A place where hard work and desire had come together to create a dream that my heart has silently chased for so long. Now, with the Covid pandemic running rampant, and the island closing, everything was up in the air.

I began to edge towards the door, my emotions reclaimed for the moment, when, against all odds, the shadow must have seen me. For without warning he abruptly changed his course and was now angling my way as if spotting prey. With some new purpose on his mind, he steadily advanced. I stood my ground, unable to duck back inside for fear he would misinterpret the action as avoidance, which I try never to do.

Ensnared, I waited for what I knew was coming. The form approaching me with obvious intent was a man I was well acquainted with and he seemed to have something he wanted to share. He's done this before, only to pass by without saying a word, but still, I waited. We have known each other for the last five years and he has set out to purposely baffle me the entire time.

He shrouds himself with an air of stoicism, mixed with quiet dispersions of his own ideas and changing theories, delivered in reverent, low tones, as though he were a mystic. Shambling toward me was a man who could run your mind in circles, and leave even the sanest man unnerved. Even more than that, he enjoys tweaking his notions to more properly fit the odd situations and strange news of the day.

His name is Randy, and I've grown to like him since we first met. He can be a bit trying and testy sometimes, but I have found that hidden under the folds of his shifting personality is a good person, with a soft heart. He's certainly an interesting guy. I would have to call him more of an acquaintance than an actual friend, as he doesn't readily embrace the term, even though I see and talk to him almost every day. Even if it's nothing more than a mumbled greeting. For reasons of his own choosing, he's invented a different sort of logic to better cope with life. We've had our share of normal conversations, but they're rare.

Randy is somewhere in his mid-thirties. I've seen him dressed in a wide array of different styles and colors from hippie to Hindu, depending on his mood, which swang the compass from day to day but was never violent. Today he was dressed in a black, open-collar shirt, unbuttoned to allow a thick mat of chest hair to sprout from the top, black board shorts, and a black straw fedora, with a black feather from a Nene curiously poking up from the hatband. With the long coat he was wearing he could have been Johnny Cash. Even the sandals he wore were black.

It was a look he chose often lately, devoid of color and lacking substance as if he saw the world that way, and I believe he did. He's revealed his fluctuating ideas to me enough over the years for me to know what topics to avoid. Otherwise, the only other option to moving the day forward is to ally and concede whatever point he was trying to make. Which is precisely what he wants, to see if he can bring you to his side. He knows exactly what he's doing and he plays the game like a seasoned pro.

He ambles over and manages to raise his head. He stares at me with faraway eyes that appear to be looking straight through me into another time. Haunted eyes. I wish I knew more of his story; I know some, but not enough to understand why he's become the introverted and suspicious character he has chosen to be. He's never been one to speak of his own life. I would often pop in a question, usually something of the background variety, only to be met with answers so vague they could belong to anyone. Or worse, a look so icy that I didn't dare suggest the matter again. He doesn't shake hands or touch fists, and he scowls at any sort of traditional greeting, so I simply pointed up and spoke.

"Hey Randy, you see the rainbow?"

"Are you kidding me?" His question was a mix of sarcasm and disgust.

"No, I'm not, looks like maybe a double. You see up above, the colors inverting?" I said.

"Dave, what are you doing out here staring at rainbows? I mean, look around you man, don't you see it, the world is swirling the drain, and you act like everything's fine, everything's normal. We're approaching some kind of global crisis here man, something I've seen coming for years, and you seem unshaken, looking at the sky. Don't you see that none of this makes sense, or…" he raises a finger and waves it around emphatically. "It's been so perfectly orchestrated, that it makes perfect sense. If you're watching. Me, I'm watching."

To be honest, I was completely shaken. It's why I was out there in the first place. I had no idea what the coming days or weeks would bring, let alone the extended lockdown for the foreseeable future. But, at the same time, I've been hearing this line from him since we met, hell it might have been our introduction. One sign after another that the world is finished, and believe me, I've tried to understand his view, but I don't think he even understands it. He'll wave his hands and ramble and contradict himself with great conviction.

"I don't know what to think, Randy, all I can seem to process are the memories and my brain won't turn those off. You know we're closing, right? Everyone is."

"Yeah, I know, I'm sorry, but it doesn't change the fact that there's some weird shit going down. You're just the fallout. This has all the feel of some type of prophecy or something. Remember what I told you about the reset?"

His beliefs run in wild directions that have no basis in fact, or most often even reality, but he nurtures and protects them like a man clinging to his last hope. One of those is the growing idea that the world will burn itself out through flood, disease, or some other cataclysm every ten thousand years or so, sweeping the Earth and wiping out all mankind, save a select few. And the cycle begins anew. Whether it's true, or not, I wouldn't know, nor would I spend any part of my day considering it, there's enough to worry about in the here and now. But Randy does.

"I don't know, Randy, you've brought this up before and I'm still not persuaded by what you're saying. Let's just relax and see what happens, I mean, there's nothing we can do now anyway. I'm not saying that it doesn't look a little bleak, but I don't think it means the end of the world, come on. You know somehow we will find a way to get through it, all of it."

"Are you serious right now? Read the signs! I've seen one military vehicle after another heading up towards the missile base, and

I overheard a guy saying that it's been that way for the last week. You think that's a coincidence? A mysterious virus, and the military massing?" He was so intense.

I thought 'massing' was a bit over the top, but I knew Randy loved big statements. The newspaper was reporting that the National Guard was pulling together their resources and preparing to enforce the upcoming shelter-in-place order. While not a comforting thought, nothing about it seemed ominous.

"I've seen it too, and I think you're making too much out of it. You're arriving at assumptions that have no basis in fact and leaping to conclusions that you know nothing about. I'm sure it's all Covid-related, I've seen a lot of big helicopters heading that way from Oahu." I didn't want to go into this.

"I might know a little more than you think, and just because I was in the Army doesn't mean I trust the government, any government. Cover-up seems to be their first, and only go-to, no man, I do not trust the government." He was a little agitated.

"So, what are you saying, that what, the world has joined in a conspiracy? I wish for once you'd get to your point, and stop driving me in circles. I've got too much on my mind to figure out your riddles" I was about to head inside.

"All I'm saying is, there's some weird shit going down, and I've been warning you about these things for a while, and now we have a situation. And we already know the Army might be involved, probably is, I saw the trucks." He said.

Now it's we.

"It's a navy base." I corrected. "Besides they're probably preparing to enforce the quarantine."

"What? You think the branch matters, F.B.I, C.I.A, Defense, whatever, and whoever it is has this under top-secret clearance. This is a free for all." His mind is moving forward, and I can see that he's still making leaps, trying to connect dots that don't exist. All in an effort to win me over.

Even with the new threat raging, he still couldn't put away the old standbys. He held them close, as if they might shield him from the real boogeyman, and explain how they not only impacted but were likely the cause of whatever was going on. The topic was old and pointless, and I had heard it so many times I could quote it. He wrapped himself in a world of cynicism and suspicion, where villainy swarmed.

Whatever hand Randy was originally dealt, something happened to him that stacked the deck against him. What that was I may never know, but psychologically, he was unable, or unwilling, to recover from it. Instead, he let the nifty little curve balls life throws buckle him at the knees. Over the years, I guess, they began to define who he is, pulling him little by little, into a landscape of his own making.

Silence for a minute, while he thinks. I take a tentative step toward the ramp that will lead me inside when he motions his arm in a displaying gesture as if he's showing me all that the world has to offer. Shifting gears and trying to prove some unknowable point, he spoke in a very soft and strained voice.

"I've tried to explain to you why I know things, but you still have no idea, do you? Let me ask you this, and I know we've discussed it before, so bear with me. What do you think about doorways, passages to an alternate world?" He asked.

"Yes, you have mentioned it, but I recall you doing most of the talking. While the topic is fascinating, I can't say that I've ever spent much time thinking about it, and I'm not convinced that they exist." I reasoned.

"Well, what do you think déjà vu is? It's a parallel memory that your body never experienced, but your mind somehow brushed up against. It means you've passed mighty close to one of those spots, and a lingering residue of some other time, like an invisible vapor, swirls around your head. One second there," he snaps his fingers, "the next gone, stopping you in its wake. It makes you almost certain that you've been there before, you've done that before. You've likely traveled near other dimensions and didn't even know it, but your mind stored it. You get it? You don't look like you get it."

No, I don't get it, fifty times at least he's shoveled this, and I still don't get it. I don't even know what there is to get. The whole argument is nothing more than fodder for some cable T.V. network. Plus, I thought we were just talking about the government. Oh, maybe they're somehow connected to the portal that brought the virus, I won't bring it up.

"I get it, Randy," I said, and walked back inside.

Ten minutes later he's back, sitting in his usual spot at the bar table closest to the back door. I walked over and set a Bud, along with a menu, down in front of him.

"Just in for a beer, or would you like something from the kitchen?" I said.

He looked at me in deep thought before answering.

"No, I'm good. Hey, I was just thinking outside, you know, with this whole thing going on around us? Nobody knows what's going to happen, what will be next, and it's got people worried, I don't know man. All the agitation going around has me on edge, you know."

"I thought you expected this or something like it, why would you feel that way? We're probably in the safest place here on an island. One that appears to be closing for the foreseeable future, I might add." I said, still shocked at the thought.

"That's just it, how long is the foreseeable future and how is it even defined? Who could know where all this is going, how this will turn out? I mean, things are already changing, tourists aren't the only people leaving the island you know. People are freaking out. I think I might be freaking out."

His glassy-eyed gaze seemed to question everything he knew, or at least thought he knew, about who he was and where he saw himself in the scheme of things. That hard outer shell he'd meticulously crafted over the years was all at once showing signs of unsurety and vulnerability, causing sudden cracks in the foundation. His lips were quivering as if he were holding back a thousand emotions, most of them completely foreign to him. Walking through the backdoor of my restaurant seemed to have flipped a switch.

Despite all my prior teachings, I wrapped an arm around his shoulders and gave him a quick squeeze and a friendly slap on the back. When I pulled away, he caught my hand and gave it a brief touch. No one would have noticed, but it was there, and the two gestures combined seemed to bring a change to him.

"You good? I don't think I've ever seen you like this before." I said in a whisper.

"I'm fine." He said, moving his body to create a proper space between us.

"You don't seem fine, you just said you were freaking out and you look like you just lost your best friend."

"I said I 'might' be freaking out. Besides, I don't have any friends and if I did, I could give a shit whether I lost them, or not."

He looked away. "That's not true, if it was, I wouldn't be sitting here, feeling this way."

"Whoa! 'Newsflash, Randy has feelings, details at eleven'." I cried in my best anchor voice.

That elicited a fleeting smile that was there and gone, but it felt like there was something more he wanted to say, some new reason that caused him to abruptly turn his attention my way outside. I hadn't been taking the conversation seriously and now something in the air was telling me that this man needed to talk to someone. It was a thought that would have never crossed my mind. Randy has always kept to himself and has never seemed to want a friendship or a close relationship with anyone for as long as I've known him. I felt bad that I was trying to lighten the mood while he was openly in the midst of some crisis.

"Hey, man, I'm sorry. I should have been more sensitive to how you were reacting to all of this. I've just never seen you like this. You want to tell me what's on your mind?" I apologized.

"No, yes…. Maybe! I don't know. I mean, I wouldn't normally."

I waited through seconds that only a few minutes ago seemed so precious, and allowed him to see that he could freely speak whatever was on his mind. I didn't know him well enough to be his confidant, but I was willing to listen and offer up my own experiences if that was what he wanted. Just when I thought he might exit the chair and leave in his usual quiet way, he surprised me.

"Look, I'm not sure what to say, but yeah, I think I want to say something." He paused.

"When I returned from overseas and left the Army, I came back to my hometown, back to live with my parents. By that time, I had formed the idea that I wanted nothing to do with people, and consequently, I began spending more and more time alone. I built a wall, brick by brick, that would keep people out. It was easy enough; the things I was interested in and spoke passionately about scared other people and made them uncomfortable. Wormholes in the desert, missing time, missing people, doorways, you know what I mean."

I nodded my head and urged him to go on.

"Well, I found it impossible to reason with anybody, let alone convince them and it led them to their own conclusions. That I needed help, that my government-sponsored tours in Afghanistan messed up my mind, that I had come back crazy. None of that is true. I mean, we're all a little crazy right, but I never saw a minute of combat and the job I had was pretty mundane. I just decided that I didn't want to be around people. I'd had enough. It wasn't hard. When I got back most of the kids I grew up with had moved on and I didn't know anybody.

Anyway, to make a long story short, it came to a head with my parents, my dad anyway, and I left. Went to California and then to Kauai. Along the way I guess I built an image of myself as a guy who didn't need anyone, didn't want to know anyone. The guy with the crazy theories. I put myself on the outskirts of society because that's where I thought I wanted to be." He stopped talking and reached for his beer.

"You're saying that's not where you really want to be?" I asked.

"I don't know. I just don't know. I do know that once this virus became real and not just some theoretical scenario to be talked about, it forced me to look at what's important to me. I've hidden from responsibilities and neglected a huge chunk of my life. It's been brought to my attention more than a few times over the years, but this week it seemed to hit me in a way I never expected. I guess what I'm getting at is my roommate moved off the island yesterday to be closer to his family. We didn't know each other when he moved in and I tried to shut him out, but he wouldn't let me. I guess we had managed some sort of friendship. Now he's gone and it has me thinking about other people I've shut out." He looked at me puzzled.

"You've had enough time on this island to get to know somebody, but instead you intentionally put up a barrier. Now, what, you think the worlds going to end, and you wish you knew your neighbor better? I don't get it." I said

"Well, yeah. And I don't expect you to get it. We've known each other for what, five years, and throughout that time, every time I see you, you're probing me with questions, asking me about this and that, like you're my biographer. Have I ever once asked you anything about your life? No. Hell, I don't even know why you moved over here from Minnesota."

"It was Michigan." I corrected.

"See, I told you. I know you'll think this sounds crazy, but after all of this, who knows where I'll be, or where you'll be, I may never see you again and I know nothing about you. I know that never seemed important before, but I guess now it does. I'd like to know at least something about your life." His eyes burrowed into me, expecting.

"You mean, like why I'm here?" I challenged.

"That's impossible. I mean, no one will ever know why any of us are here, or how for that matter, but that's for a different conversation. But yes, here on Kauai. What made you pick up, and move your life." he said.

"Well, it's interesting that you of all people would ask me that because whenever I see you lately, you've barely mumbled a complete sentence. This is probably the most we've talked in what, a month, two months, and I still don't get it."

"I've been going through a phase. Look, I know a few people, but I have never bothered to get to know any of them better. Ever. Most think I'm weird, and that's the way I want it because it's easier than getting involved. But lately, I don't know, something's changing, I feel this forgotten need to connect."

I could see the idea was causing him some anxiety, but despite that fact, he was the most comfortable I had ever seen him. Even his proclamations outside were delivered with less fervor.

"Well, I can tell you we didn't pick up our life and move it, we simply started over. Sheri and I realized that you only live once, and we committed to living where our hearts wanted us to be. I guess, I'm not sure what you're asking, what you want me to say." I didn't sense any angst in his voice, or a sermon coming about everywhere, and nowhere. Yet, in all honesty, I barely knew this man.

It got me thinking, however, that Sheri and I have been asked a lot over the years, meeting as many people as we do, essentially the same question in a variety of different ways. Answered by us in bits and pieces as the occasion warranted. People by nature are curious and I guess, Randy, somewhere in that shell he created, was no exception.

"I don't cozy up to people, you know that, but you're the closest thing I've got to an actual friend, and I know nothing about you. You told me once that you left everything behind and took a five-thousand-mile leap of faith. I've known you too long to not know at least that, and while I'm not making apologies for who I am, I guess, I want to change that. I know you think I'm attempting to clear my conscience or something, and maybe I am, but that's not all." His candor came as a total surprise to me. Considering our conversation outside, I was caught off guard by the openness of his request.

"I guess I've never really thought too much about it, it could take a while, and besides, I'm just a regular guy. I'm not sure what you'll get out of it."

"Look man, you might say something that hits on just what I need. Your experiences, whatever they are, might help me see through mine. I'm carrying a weight that I don't want to carry anymore, a guilt that I've dragged around for too long. I have feelings that I don't know how to process. I've never shared it, but I respect you, Dave. When I saw you outside, I thought I'd come over and harass you, maybe make myself feel better, but I think there was more to it. I could see that you were as lost as I am and when I followed you inside and saw the empty restaurant, something broke. The phone call from my mother started it." He said, almost in a whisper.

"You've talked to your family; you didn't mention that. How was it?"

"I let it go to message, just like all the other times, but in the end, she asked me if I was ready to come home. I've been thinking a lot about it, and I guess, maybe I am. So, will you share your story?"

I didn't think I had much to give, especially to Randy, but he seemed to need this, and if I could do anything to help him move forward, then I wanted to do that. Besides, somebody should know we were here, and why. But is this a story I wanted to share with him of all people, and in how much detail, and where do I start? I guess it's not much different from telling a curious stranger at the bar. I finally resigned and moved closer to the table.

I looked around the restaurant, knowing at that time of day, under normal conditions, the place would be about half full. Today it sat open for the last time, but empty. I pulled out the chair across from him and sat down, silently looking off into nothing. Gathering the wool my grandmother would say. I was peering into a past, that was for me easier forgotten, not overly painful, just easier forgotten.

I had no idea what he was expecting, why he was suddenly so interested, and why it even mattered to me that he was, but for some strange reason, it did. Randy needed something, neither of us was completely sure what that was, or even certain that I could provide it. He came in seeking a friend, something that was clearly new to him, and I wanted to be that friend. I looked at him, and he looked at me, and I started from the beginning.

## CHAPTER 2

# My father's desire

For thirty years I woke up each weekday, threw on a fresh uniform, poured a cup of coffee for the road, and sped off in a morning haze to a job that I despised with every fiber of my being. That might be a bit overstated, but not by much. I had found success throughout the years. I even had a few moments worth celebrating. But it never took away the dread of waking up with that day ahead of me. What makes little sense, considering my overall lack of interest, is that I had gotten pretty good at it, eventually demanding perfection, not just from myself, but the people around me, and in all those hateful years I rarely missed a day.

I had spent the bulk of my life as a licensed plumber, and while the trade itself required a collection of skills that went beyond the mechanical abilities of most, it never once fulfilled the life I wanted. What that life was, I ultimately didn't know, but I had dreams that I kept safely locked away in the recesses of my mind, unable to bring them into the light because I had no idea how to articulate them. It seemed I was destined for the road in front of me, the one my father was preparing, and a deviation from that road to chase something else was an option I didn't have the luxury of entertaining.

The hard work end of things never weighed in on my feelings for the job, or the career I reluctantly chose, although it took me a little time to come around. My dad used to say that I'd run from a shovel like my hair was on fire. I was never really sure how those two things went together, I mean, wouldn't you run from anything if your hair was on fire, but that was the old man, and how I never could make sense of him. But early on in my young life, he was right.

I pissed him off a lot, my dad. I do know that. I was lazy as a teenager, and while I had an active mind, it was too often scattered and unfocused. It made us adversaries through my teen years, neither one of us ever really knowing the other, and it hasn't changed much, even now. It was a strange yin and yang, where on one hand I feared even the smallest conversation with the man, while on the other, I wanted so desperately for him to notice me, to see that I was worth something, to make him proud. I failed most of the time, with him anyway.

I spent my late teen years and into my twenties, learning life the hard way, never quite able to dodge the quick jab or the sneaky left hook delivered from all the unseen angles, but I managed to get my hands up once, or twice. I was battling with myself mostly; why couldn't I speak out the few ambitions and ideas I had of my own desires for life? Why was I so afraid to let my father down, when it was so painfully obvious that he had no interest in me?

Without a plan for what lies ahead, any future is nearly impossible to chase. My father had narrowed my vision over the years until it was whittled down to his one myopic view; that I would work for him, and eventually down the road, take over the business that he had built. I was, in all honesty, afraid of stepping out and finding my own path, let alone creating one.

Late in my senior year of high school, I was sitting with a group of friends around our usual table at Mr. Taco, when two of them started talking about college, the fall semester, and how life-changing it was going to be. Everyone was chattering all at once about the future, what they ultimately wanted to become, and where they would go from there. I laughed with them, fist-bumped and hand-slapped, and celebrated their plans and designs for life. I sat there amidst my classmates, knowing that I was strapped into the passenger seat of my own life. Rocketing to a future that at that point, I wasn't even sure I wanted, but knowing from what's inside of me, was utterly powerless to stop.

Memories like these remind me that peer pressure is hard enough at any age and it comes and goes as circumstances change, but family pressure is inescapable. I knew early on where my life was heading and I couldn't seem to change the direction. My parents, as much as I love them, never once put forth the idea of college for me to consider. It seemed to be well established that I was heading for an apprenticeship with my father, and what I may have wanted otherwise, wasn't deemed an option. He had it in mind that I would be the heir to his company, and I wasn't born to rock the boat.

I try not to waste much time on what if, and what would I change if I could do it all over again. Of course, I'd change a dozen things, but as it turned out, those things changed me, helped me see and understand, not just myself, but everything else around me. Sure, I've burned a few bridges. Who hasn't? It's part of being on the battlefield and making a safe retreat, but I've also built a lot of them too. The lessons I've learned throughout my life have shaped who I am, and while some have carved everlasting scars, I like to believe I've come out okay. Some may argue.

As I continued to mature, I was overtaken by a world that was moving way too fast and I kicked, fought, and stumbled my way through it like a wino chased by his own demons. When I think back on the mistakes I've made, and the people I know I've hurt, all the things I should have said, or should have done, I can see that I was struggling to find balance in so many areas of my life. I can also see now, that I was most of all, troubled with finding myself. I spent a lot of time groping in the dark, reaching for anything that would anchor me to a place, that would explain where I am, and where I fit.

The course of my life has taken a few detours in its silent quest to one day reach the dream that has ruminated in the back of my mind for so long. Left to rot on those varied pathways, with all the blind turns and dark alleys, the smooth four-lane highways, and the brightly lit avenues, are scattered pieces of another life. It took me longer than most people, I guess, to understand who I was, and finally, be comfortable with who I am. In some ways that fight continues, but through it all, I think I've learned to shed almost all of the insecurity, anxiety, and self-doubt that surrounded so much of my life.

Most of those emotions have been with me from a young age and seemed to stem from my relationship with my father. He had made up his mind early that I was born a plumber, third generation, and he was going to teach me everything I needed to know, so I'd be ready someday to take over the business. I was ten at the time. I guess even he had his dreams. I, however, would have easily settled for anything else. I appreciate what my father tried to do for me. I just wish that in a landscape so filled with possibilities, he would have helped me find the keys that opened other doors.

Michigan has always been my home, I was raised amid long, dark winters, and summer camping trips that were scheduled to follow the old man's softball tournaments. I've seen almost every inch of that sublime, and radiant peninsula, from the endless miles of waterfront bordering the great lakes to the deep and noble pine forests that blanket the north. There's a sprinkling of big cities laid out here and there across the mitten, giving rise to thoughts of civilization between the vast expanses of corn, soybeans, barns, and silos that dot the open farmland from shore to shore. Whether it's hunting for whitetail, fishing the thousands of streams for trout and walleye, or world-class skiing, golf, dining, and entertainment, Michigan has it all, and sometimes all in the same weekend.

I suppose I should consider myself lucky to have been born into a place that makes it so easy to call home. A place where leaving never crosses the mind of most of the people who make their lives there. And in a lot of ways I do feel fortunate. Except, I never really felt at home, I longed for a life outside of where I was. I felt displaced. It was my home for nearly five decades, and never once did I ever feel like I belonged there.

The year after I was born, the Tigers completed an unlikely comeback and won the 1968 World Series. My mom holds to her claim that I watched every game from a blanket on the floor, and only complained when the Cardinals scored. It doesn't immediately come to mind. What I do remember was her constant presence as I grew up. Not smothering, or lording, just a feeling of security, comfort, and trust, the very definition of home. She loved baseball, and her passion for it made me love it. We shared that until the day she died. It created a bond that went beyond the game and bred an atmosphere of easy conversation and comfortable silence. I miss that.

Before I entered the world, my parents had decided early, that my mother would quit her job at the bank and they would forgo the added cost of a babysitter. I figured she must have enjoyed the new job, because she stayed on to also raise my sister, and in time, with the neighborhood growing, she started a daycare.

My parents made sacrifices that I knew nothing about to allow that to happen and had learned to fit their lives accordingly. The upside was that my mom was there, bandaging skinned knees, making us breakfast, packing our lunches, and sending us off to school. And she would be there at the end to hear about who did what to who, and who said what to who. I never knew any different.

When it came to discipline in our family, the role seemed to lend itself quite naturally to my mother's no-bullshit, in-your-face personality, and it made no difference to her where we happened to be. I was dragged along on a shopping trip to J.C. Penny once, and only once, when she had clearly reached her threshold of patience for whatever I was dishing out. She grabbed my hand and whisked me away to the men's department, where I found myself standing in front of the belt rack, and my mother plucking one off the peg. The mere threat was enough to shut me up.

She was the judge and jury, and the sentencing stage was in her hands as well. Penalties ranged anywhere from a stern reprimand to threats, confiscations, and corporal punishment. While the option of a quick smack on the ass was never off the table, she usually preferred incarceration of various lengths. Time spent in my bedroom without any of the modern devices so many kids have now. If that wasn't bad enough, my temporary cell had one window, and my friends took pleasure in coming to it to let me know everything they planned to do that day. Very helpful.

The twenty-inch Magnavox, which doubled as a piece of heavy furniture, and somehow managed to occupy an entire wall, held no interest for my young mind. Those three fuzzy and glitchy channels, couldn't possibly compare to the world of imagination and wonder that was waiting to be found on my bike. Most often those journeys took me well outside the limits of where I was allowed to go. Trouble arose when those critical boundaries were crossed, both physical, as well as the ones that float around the ether, the unwritten laws that every family possesses.

I was never on time, I was rarely where I said I was, and I was usually with someone I was told not to hang out with, so I was always testing and pushing those boundaries. It was only a matter of time before I would push too far, and have to face my mother, who did her best to shape my character, even if another wooden spoon lay broken on the floor, or later when my car was impounded in the garage and no release date in sight. I guess that's why I had so much respect for her as I grew older, because early in life she was my rudder and compass, and in her way, impacted the man I would become.

My father was just the opposite. He would give me this divided stare like he was trying to figure out a complicated math problem that was somehow related to the bowling league. He was rarely the keynote speaker at whatever lecture was taking place at the dining-room table, never bothering to chip in his two cents on the topic or outline any values that could be gained from it. No, he was more likely to just sit there smoking, a beer in front of him, unreadable and unknowable, the embodiment of silence, lost in a world called home that he had no idea how to navigate.

My mom kept her feelings in the open and her temperature was easy to read. She made sure you knew she was there and what was on her mind, and while she could be embarrassing at times, I loved her for that. I had a bond with my mother that I just couldn't have with my father. With her, I was free to talk about anything, no topic was off-limits. And when the time came, and it came often, she wasn't afraid to tell me how foolish I was being, or how wrong I was. My mom was bold and up-front with her opinions, and it didn't matter if you were there, or not.

"Did I tell you Jean's daughter is having a baby?" She'd say.

"No, I never heard."

"I don't think she even has a boyfriend. And she used to bitch about how I raised you kids."

Yes, I'm biased, but I had a great mom. One minute she could be telling you the recipe for a dip she just made, and the next explaining the infield fly rule. She loved camping and bonfires, road trips, and Sunday doubleheaders, but mostly she enjoyed the home life and messing around in the kitchen. I see a lot of her in me as I've grown older.

I wish I knew why I was so on edge around my father. It stayed that way throughout my life and seemed to affect every relationship I ever had, like I was, somehow, forever stained with the ocher of his indifference toward me. I still wasn't fully committed to the idea of working for him, even though it was one of the few things he ever addressed in my direction, but by default, I had convinced myself that I was ultimately left with no choice. To my old man, the plumbing trade was like hitting the lottery, he had found his calling and decided that I had found mine. But I hadn't. Yet, there I was, set to be his apprentice in what he called an exciting new world.

The relationship between the two of us struggled when I was young, in fact, most of the time I rarely saw him, and when I did, he didn't have much to say to me. He was the alleged head of our family, although, everybody knew who that really was, but he kept his appearances brief. Even if I caught a rumor that he was home, he was likely next door, or down the street. My dad placed a high priority, much higher than I could ever rise to, on the stable of friends he kept and turned his attention to enough outside activity to keep him busy year-round.

If there was a recreational league to be a part of, my father would join three. Bowling, golf, softball, horseshoes, you name it, he was there. We had our moments of connection, like the time he coached my little league baseball team or led our pack during my Cub Scout years, but they were few. I came to see him as more of a minor presence in my life than an actual contributor to it, at least in the ways that mattered to me. Yes, he did put a roof over our heads and food on the table, but I can't recall ever having a heart-to-heart conversation with him, about anything, at any stage of my life, and believe me, I had plenty of need for it. He just wasn't the type of person that made me feel comfortable opening up to or asking for advice. The truth is, he made me insecure just being around him. If he ever sensed that, he never made a move to change it.

I remember the summer I turned sixteen. My father had traded a plumbing job for a worn-out seventy-three Chevy Nova hatchback, and though it would take a lot of work, he said, he was offering it to me as my first car. We may have hugged, I doubt it, but I was excited and he knew it. There was a lot of rust and a few holes to patch. The vinyl top had a rip in it, and more than a few things looked like they didn't fit together right. But the interior was remarkably clean. When it finally started, the engine sounded like a little tinkering was required. Of course, he had a guy for that. My dad and I filled our nights and weekends for the next month, in the garage scraping, sanding, and rebuilding the body of that car.

The man used skills I didn't even know he had. We rarely spoke, other than for him to tell me what to do, or demonstrate how to do it. When it came to conversation, I had no idea where to begin, or what to say to him, and he apparently felt the same way. I was, of course, edgy around him. His quiet and chilly demeanor towards me left me with nothing to say and made me nervous, so consequently, we spent much of that time in silence, unless one of his friends showed up, which was inevitable. Thankfully the radio, or the running of the air compressor, filled the void.

We spent weeks working on that car and after all the body-work, engine work, and a new paint job from Earl Scheib, I had my first ride. I loved that car. I waxed it, I babied it, I jacked up the rear end with air shocks, and even threw some chrome on, here and there. I had possibly the coolest car in the school parking lot that fall until I hit black ice the following winter and my inexperience caused me to slide it into a tree. Luckily the stout pine saved me from the picture window I was barreling towards. I came out fine, the car, however, did not. My old man scarcely took notice of my condition, but he sure was concerned about that car.

The work we did in the garage that spring is surprisingly one of my great memories from my teen years. As uncomfortable as it was, it had its own rewards, but as you might otherwise expect, the shared experience did nothing to draw my father and me closer together. It's uncanny how many hours we spent together, neither one of us willing to offer anything or make an attempt to bridge the gap.

I look back with some miles behind me and I can't help but think that I blew a great opportunity to break my shell and really try to know my dad. It's hard to explain, but he didn't breed that same atmosphere of open conversation that I had with my mother. But I was sixteen, and the thought of reaching across that divide and making a connection seemed impossible. Like Evil Knevel jumping the Snake River, and that didn't turn out so well.

I guess I never really knew the man. He was my dad, but he showed little ability and even less interest in fulfilling that role. If he was ever intrigued by the idea of a healthy father-son relationship, he never let on, and probably didn't know how to get there. I concluded later, that in the end, his friends were more important than his family. Look, I'm no parent, and if I was, I sure as hell wouldn't be a father of the year candidate myself, I'm just relating my own views as I saw them. He made little effort to know, or understand who I was, so I mostly avoided him.

He was quiet in his own way, he wasn't prone to violence, outbursts of anger, or sweeping mood changes, but his overall lack of attention and disinterest in the things that mattered to me, or the way I felt, hurt nonetheless. He was very self-centered, and while not a driven man, was at the same time, self-interest driven. Still is. Maybe his father treated him the same way. I don't know, I never knew his dad or much about his upbringing, but it has a ring of truth because when it came to me, my dad so often simply had other things to do.

I'm not sure how he ever thought we could work together. Our relationship had been awkward for years, a sort of passing in the halls feeling that only seemed to intensify when we were around each other for too long. I don't think my dad ever took the time to wonder about it, or if he had considered how it would play out in a work environment. I knew it was going to take a tremendous effort on my part because I didn't want to be there in the first place.

My sister was the shining star as far as my father was concerned, the one that could do no wrong, and was bound for higher things. Any pride that the old man would allow himself to show, was usually directed at her. They seemed to share a bond that so many fathers and daughters form, a closeness that I never knew with him but found with my mother in earnest. She had earned a rare place in my father's heart, and at times I was envious. She was born four years after me, and although there was an age gap, we had a good relationship, until she hit her senior year of high school and went a different way.

Somehow, on a limited but manageable income, my parents had been setting aside a fund for my sister to entertain thoughts on college, which she did. I was never apparently figured into the mix, hell I'd never even heard about the so-called fund until she was handed the award. I was left a little shaken, wondering what I might have done with that opportunity, if pushed in that direction. The degree in Home-Ec, or whatever she majored in, was consumed in the maelstrom of marriage, babies, dogs, and scheduled moves from one city to another. She married a military man who adhered to the same newly found spiritual teachings as she did. So, while he delivered the income, she delivered the grandkids.

Her views of life and how each of us should live it are different from mine, and she abides by a certain and strict code. At an influential age, she was taken in and swallowed up by a flock whose teachings made her insufferable to those who stood outside of her beliefs. She didn't get along well with my mom after that, always dropping not-so-subtle hints that she needed to change her ways. Because I couldn't seem to stay married, in her eyes, I became the black sheep, no longer spoken to for fear I might corrupt the children.

As my high school years drew to a close, the excitement of finally graduating was quickly tempered by the fact that it was time to start working for the old man. He loved the idea that his son would be following in his footsteps. It blinded him to what was in front of him, and it didn't matter what I wanted. There was no courage in me to tell him that I had no interest in this. Instead, I set my mind to it and decided that if this was the path, then I was determined to somehow succeed. It took a while to finally figure that out, but eventually, I did.

My dad owned a one-man plumbing outfit in the downtown area, which he later turned into an efficient four-man operation. The name of the shop was on the front door when he bought the place, and he never changed it. He had recently sold his first company to his partner and was now starting over again, only this time as a sole proprietor. I wasn't mature enough to respect what he had done at the time, to me it felt like a prison.

"One day your son will own all this." He said as we stood in the back room, organizing inventory.

"I don't know if I'll ever have a son." I remind him. Hell I wasn't even married yet.

"Someday you will, and…well…!" He motions around the room as if showing me what I could win in the showcase showdown if I just pick the right answer.

I understood that my father was presenting me with what he considered a well-reasoned and well-rounded opportunity, but I wasn't ready to embrace it yet, and I sure as hell wasn't going to make it the first option on my future son's list of career choices. I think I would push him as far away from that shabby backroom as

I could and encourage, possibly demand, that he chase down the life that exceeds his dreams, and if it turns out to be the plumbing business, it will at least be his decision. That power was mine all along if I had just learned how to use it. Or if I could somehow get past my fear.

Books have been a part of my life as far back as I can remember. I have always been a reader. From history to fiction, to biographies, I was filled with other ambitions and my own desires for life. I just wasn't sure how to define them, or more importantly, how to get there if I could. It seemed no one would show me. I wasn't a dumb kid, just lacking self-confidence. So I couldn't understand why I was letting someone who I felt like I barely knew, and for sure wasn't entirely comfortable around, lead me to my future.

The easiest answer is to say that I didn't have a choice, that my path was already set, as if I were part of some royal bloodline. To some extent that would be true because that's the way I felt at the time, and how I saw things with my limited vision. I was more concerned with disappointing my mother than I was with fulfilling my father's desires. The truth is actually worse and speaks to the person I was at the time. I simply didn't have the internal make-up to go against what my father wanted. Even at that young age, with my whole life ahead of me, I just couldn't see anything else. I couldn't look beyond the illusion that my father had built.

Resigned to the fact that it had become my destiny, I still spent the first couple of years working for him in a constant battle between what he wanted, and my utter lack of interest in giving it to him. It went on that way for a few years. My eagerness for the job seemed to come and go as frequently as the phases of the moon. Somehow, through all the riding around as my father's apprentice, I had steadily acquired the knowledge and gained enough understanding of the trade to allow me to pass the state licensing exam.

I knew I had done well and as I waited for the results to come in the mail, he decided that I should start taking service calls on my own. After three years I guess he was ready, if not exactly confident, to stake his reputation on me. I hadn't given him much to base that idea on, but we were at a point where I had to move forward. I had to prove that I could do this on my own. I knew enough about myself to know that I was good at the job, that I had learned well and knew what I was doing. But, in a short time, a letter would arrive announcing that I was a professional, and that, I wasn't sure I was ready for.

I remember the first time he handed me a work order and gave me his lecture on what he expected. I practically ran out the door before he could change his mind. I left the office as if I were breaking out of prison, with an equal measure of fear, panic, and euphoria, disappearing into a labyrinth of side streets and alleys that led to the highway. The ride, with its new-found independence, was exhilarating, slashing across town, adrenalin pumping, to an address where untold possibilities could easily go awry. Armed only with my limited training to tip the balance.

Within a week he was encouraged enough to buy another service truck and we spent a day setting it up. It was now up to me to put into practice the things I'd learned, and gain my own experience. There was freedom in that. I had a few victories and ran into twice as many problems. I found the origins of a mysterious leak that baffled two other companies. I backed one of our vans into the other, I mowed down a fencepost, things like that. I learned my trade, and I got better at it every day, every year, but I couldn't get out of my father's shadow.

To his credit, he put up with a lot of shit from me that no one else would have. Maybe that was one of the few advantages of being his son. I cut out of work early quite often to play golf, wearing out the excuse that I thought we were done for the day. I took a few lunch breaks that took up the rest of the day and beyond, leaving him in the dark as to where I was. I did a lot of things that neither advanced our relationship nor earned his trust.

I couldn't seem to take the job seriously, and because he was my father, I took it for granted that it would always be there, whether I wanted it, or not. It wasn't how I had set out to treat him, or his business, I just allowed it to evolve that way. I guess I just didn't care enough to see what I was doing. He flipped a light on for me when he told me once that if I wasn't his son, he'd have fired me a long time ago. It's one of the few things he said to me that I've always remembered, that I ever really took to heart. His comment, so direct, and so personal, opened my eyes to the fact that I may have thought I was a good plumber, but my failure to grow up, to become a man who embraced integrity, had made me a terrible employee.

After eight years of working for my dad, I had put all that nonsense behind me, and was approaching my twenty-seventh birthday. Over the previous six months, I had been weighing the pros and cons of leaving and making a lateral move to another company. He had been mentioning the future of the business a lot lately and was in the beginning stages of working out his own math. A partnership with a sliding percentage scale, some form of profit-sharing, and adding my name to the title of the property, were just a few ideas he was kicking around. The only thing missing was his exit strategy, which I assumed didn't exist.

The day came when I had moved beyond just thinking about leaving, and I had taken a job offer with a rival company, which, in my mind, was easily settled. I just couldn't find the heart to tell him. I knew what his designs were. Hell, I've known since I was a child that I was destined to be a plumber, and follow in his footsteps. I had to come clean so he could prepare for what was next. It wasn't easy, considering all the things I'd put him through early on, and all the time he invested into training me, but this wasn't my future. When I finally tried to give it a voice, it did not go as I had planned.

On the day in question, I had come into work a little late due to a dentist appointment. I planned it that way thinking my dad would be in the back by then, organizing his truck. Sitting at her desk was his long-time secretary, who, by the reproachful look she was giving me, had pieced together what I was about to do. At the table where the work orders were sorted was another associate of my father. I had seen him around from time to time and he appeared to be filling out what looked like new hire paperwork.

In his small cubicle, my dad asked me if there was something I wanted to tell him. I said there was, but now might not be the best time. I could feel the eyes of the other two people in the room trailing me as I came in the door, to where my father was sitting, rummaging through a parts catalog. I took a glance around the room and I could see them quickly turning away, confirming my suspicions that this surprising turn of events was not unexpected. Something in my father's stance and the look on his face told me that he already knew. I told him that I'd like to sit down and explain later when we were alone and talk about it after work.

Since we had never once laid our hearts open to each other, it would take every ounce of my fledgling character for me to demonstrate how I had come to this decision, and why. It's been my belief throughout my life, that had I been able to do that, have the conversation that I had rehearsed and practiced well into the night, it might have changed the way we saw each other. It seems like such a small moment, and completely contrary to the situation, but I think it could have halted the direction of our relationship.

My father stayed true to himself, however, when he said he didn't need that, I could go now. He said there wasn't anything to explain. It is what it is. I thought, and not for the first time, that I couldn't believe this man was my father. Yes, I had caused him plenty of grief in the past, but for my part, I had moved beyond that to become a model employee in the company. I had no idea where we would go from there. Everything I wanted to say, everything I wanted him to know, died on my lips and has never been spoken. He dismissed me to take a phone call and I left.

## CHAPTER 3

# Same path different road

For the first time in more than eight years, I wouldn't be following the same predictable route that had carried me to work for a third of my life. I wouldn't be stopping for doughnuts and standing around a small office drinking coffee, waiting for my dad to sort out the day's work orders. I would likely, no longer be playing darts at noon, or leaving for a tee time at three either. But more importantly, if I'm honest, I would also be without my father's experience and knowledge to guide me.

It had now been a week since my abrupt departure as my father's employee and I had neither seen nor heard from him throughout that time. I think he figured I'd show up at his desk again, begging him for my job back because it was just too tough out there. He had told me a few times that I probably wouldn't last long at another company. My father seemed to think I had it pretty cushy where I was and that I somehow couldn't manage the job once I stepped from the cover of his protective wing. I was about to test the waters and find out if he was wrong.

I got a taste of the outside world when I pulled into the parking lot on my first day at the new job. It was one of the few times that I actually couldn't wait to get there. New place, new start, I guess. I looked around and learned very quickly that the guy wasn't messing around. My new boss was berating somebody just outside the overhead door. Turns out it was one of my co-workers and I was assigned to ride with him for the day. Having said all that he needed to say, the man in charge turned to me and shook my hand as he led me through the door and into the warehouse. Introductions were made, the other three plumbers went back to their duties, and I was left standing with Mark, who flipped off the boss as he turned to go back into his office.

He showed me around the warehouse, pointed out where things were stored, and then led me over to his service truck. He opened the back of a twelve-foot cube van and gestured for me to look around. I was speechless. I couldn't believe anyone could operate with that much confusion. Parts and pieces of everything, both old and new, were everywhere, mostly all over the floor. Two rows of shelving on either side appeared to be of no use to him, as they lay empty, and forgotten, save for a few discarded boxes.

This is one of those trades that require a mountain of supplies, and there's no possible way to carry everything, so the challenge is to organize the innumerable inventory of materials that is most commonly used. It didn't look like Mark was up to that challenge. The back of his truck was in total disarray. I knew instantly that he was clearly not trained by my father. He added a few more items to the mix and closed the door without a word. We jumped in the truck with a stack of work orders, and off we went.

"What was that about back there," I said.

"Same old thing, I seem to find new ways to piss him off." He replied. "I'm sure you'll find out soon enough. Everyone does."

I thought that if he kept his service truck in better order that he might have a better chance to eliminate a few of those ways, but I didn't mention that to him.

The company was owned and operated by two cousins, passed down from generation to generation where it landed in the hands of these two. Tim was the youngest and my immediate boss. He wasn't long out of college and in his office hung the ornately framed degree he had earned along the way. Next to it was an equally displayed plumbing license that he somehow gained without ever spending a day in the field. That earned him an unspoken lack of respect from some of the guys who worked their tails off for it. I wasn't one of them, I had enough issues of my own without pointing a finger at someone else. For all the years I worked for Tim, he and I never had a problem. In fact, I probably taught him twice as much as he ever knew before.

For the next week, I rode around with each guy and got an idea of how the company wanted things done. It was on a couple of these rides that I got to know Carl, the oldest of our group and a three-year apprentice. At forty-one, he was about to take the exam, which was a three-part, eight-hour marathon. I gave him some pointers and outlined things to absolutely not forget because two-thirds of the test is hands-on fieldwork. After spending enough time with him to form an opinion, I didn't hold out much hope for his passing.

He would come to work often, smelling like he hadn't left the bar long before, eyes red, not exactly ready to embrace the day. He had a quick temper at these times, and when he was pissed off, he'd snap. It was best to be somewhere else. He hadn't been there very long before I came aboard, and I had already made up my mind that he wouldn't be working there much longer. I think that by hiring me when he did, Tim was hedging his bet in the same direction.

In the short time I had been there, I witnessed him in the parking lot twice, yelling at his wife. He'd also been in several heated arguments with the office staff, and he quarreled regularly with Joe, our most experienced guy. I wasn't sure how he got the job in the first place, or how he managed to still keep it. It was Tim's attempt to help out a friend of a friend that never materialized the way he had hoped. Carl took to the job as well as I ever did, and seemed to have more passion for it than I could ever begin to muster. He just couldn't control his mood swings.

The end for him came at seven-thirty, one morning, a month after I started working there. I was in the warehouse, going about my normal routine when a huge commotion erupted in the area where the trucks were parked.

"Fuck you, I don't have anything that belongs to you."

"You might if you'd just take a look; I think I saw it in your van this morning."

"I don't have any of your shit, man. What's your problem anyway? Why are you such an asshole to me? And why are you going through my stuff? How do I know you didn't take something from me?" Carl was instantly running hot.

"Relax, I was just asking, maybe you picked it up by mistake." Joe, always the peacemaker.

I was coming around to the understanding that one of Joe's hand tools, a wrench of some kind maybe, had come up missing, and he was sure that it had migrated to Carl's truck.

"Don't tell me to relax, you're the one that better relax, and be lucky I don't come over there and knock your fuckin teeth in. You and your bullshit."

"What's going on with you guys." I started to say when Carl abruptly cut me off and turned his glare towards me.

"It's not your fucking business." Duly noted, I slipped away to watch the fireworks from a sheltered location.

In the next two seconds, Carl starts throwing tools in Joe's direction, crashing and tinkling around his feet, and sliding under the van like some crazy hail storm produced by a demented foundry.

"Is this yours, you son of a bitch? How about this one, prick? No? I guess I don't see anything that belongs to an arrogant asshole." Carl fired tools and obscenities with equal vigor until he seemed to run out of both.

Meanwhile, Tim had come out of his office and stood gawking at the scene for a full minute, looking more like a shocked menswear mannequin than the figure he was billed as. He recovered quickly enough and brought the two of them into his office for a chat. I had a feeling how this one was going to turn out. Kevin was terminated, and I never saw him again. As we had all left by the time a judgment was handed down, the news came to me in the form of extra work orders that day.

To this point, I had never really worked with other people, it was always just my father and me. So, interacting with co-workers was something new, and a different experience than what I had known before. It was interesting to be a part of a blend of personalities that came together as one unit. Together, our new team formed a group of four guys that gave a shit about every part of their job and did it at a high level.

We earned each other's respect every day and built a lot of pride in our work. That all came together after Carl left, like some element of failure was removed. We were friends, the four of us that worked there, and for over fifteen years no one left, and nobody new came in. I think about Carl sometimes, no matter how much you figure you can teach someone, or how badly you need a guy to fill a position, this was one of those times where a piece just didn't fit the puzzle.

I guess I was the first to leave. Without the common bond of work and career, I discovered that friendships have a way of fading, even those forged through the span of several years. We had a good run, but things change. Life changes. You wake up to the fact that time marches on, relentlessly, and no matter how bad you want it to, it never slows down. So, my wife and I came to a decision, and we started making plans and setting in motion the future we wanted. Instead of sitting around talking about it, we began to act and plan, and fill entire notebooks…but, I'm getting a little ahead of myself.

## CHAPTER 4

# Dreaming amidst a hurricane

When I was young, while storming through magazines for a school project, I came across a bright, colorful photograph. It was a row of coconut palms, their slender, curving trunks snaking into a sky so blue that the ocean behind them was forced to change its color. Not to be outdone, a sea of emerald, sparkled and danced to an endless horizon. The entire scene was so alive, so real, that I expected to feel the light breeze that moved every frond waft across my face.

I was left gaping at the most amazing thing I'd ever seen. My teenage mind was exploding with the idea of a life surrounded by those trees and that ocean. I couldn't begin to comprehend a bearing to that future, whatever it was, but I carefully tore out the image and kept it neatly tucked between the pages of *Treasure Island* for a very long time.

In the beginning, after the palm trees had revealed themselves, all I could think about were things like living near the ocean, reading in a hammock, and enjoying the year-round summer. Probably chicks in bikinis, too. As I got older, not matured, we're still waiting on that, but older, those dreams incorporated my love of cocktails, cooking, and people. Pretty soon I had a whole fantasy of my own open-air beer garden, umbrella drinks, and a home in the tropics, that was making up the white noise in the vast background of my mind. That absurd vision, in such contrast to the fated life I found myself wandering in, only added to my restless and unsettled path. One which like a hurricane, has left a trail of broken things and scattered expectations in its hazardous wake.

My life continued its roller coaster even as I approached forty. I guess going through the marriage and divorce process a few times has a way of doing that. The good, in a tight race, was marginally outdistancing the bad, but I was letting life lead me, which I was slow to discover is never a good idea. Life needs guidance, direction, and constant course adjustments. On its own, it has no clue where it's going. Left unchecked, it will flounder and drift, and leave you wondering where the hell twenty years went, and why am I still circling in the same spot.

Two thoughts ran spiritedly through my head, like squirrels on curtains. The first was the idea that my life was stuck in the same endless pattern, passing landmarks that were all too familiar, and following the same bogus directions that I knew would only lead to dead ends. I wanted something else. I wanted so desperately to roll the dice on a dream before it was too late.

Shouldering through the door right behind this desire is the fact that I know it's just a fantasy, my life's dream. I know this because the very short list of intimates I've ever dared share it with, even just as a ruse, has told me so. No one I had met, including the ones I married, would take up the subject as anything more than just daydreaming, and they certainly were in no rush to pack up the car and begin a new life somewhere near the Equator.

I guess what my heart was searching for through a trio of failed marriages, was a partner who was willing to reach out for something more. Someone who shared and understood my longing for a life beyond what we were living, and like an oil-soaked torch, was just waiting for that spark to light the way. But I never found it, and the eventual blame for these failures has fallen at my feet more than once, and it's well deserved, or so I've come to accept.

So, on I went, crashing through the life I was given, trying to limit the damage, and keep it on a heading that was, if not true north, then at least something close to acceptable. All I had wanted for most of my life was to be somewhere else, to be forever out of my father's shadow, and it clouded the view of what was around me. I poured myself into work and selfishly allowed certain things to go untended until they eventually fell apart.

Through it all, I had yet to fully mature. I let my strange yearning for a completely different life, corrode the one I was living. I knew my life was destined to stay the course that it was on, and I was coming to accept that. But I never could quite put away that dream, that secret desire for a tropical place, a palm tree forever in view, and that warm, gentle breeze blowing across my skin. The proud owner of a kitschy little tropical shack, where the drinks are cold and colorful, and an island band plays into the night.

It took more courage than I possessed to attempt that leap from the known to the unknown, and I know I would have never done it alone. Those thoughts and dreams I kept locked away because that's what they were, my own musings on a life no one could ever understand. Because my friends and the people that surrounded me knew me as a tradesman, they couldn't imagine that I would want anything more than my own plumbing outfit.

For them, it was a logical progression in the scheme of life for who they thought I was.

One night, a little while before I met Sheri, I was sitting in a camp chair on the back deck of my house, working through a bottle of Jim Beam and searching for satellites. My neighbor, Jeff, was there. He lived up the street with his wife and two kids, and we had just finished expanding the very deck we were sitting on. We pointed out a few stars and planets, and in the silence, he asked me where I'd like to be in ten years.

I thought about it for a second, knowing what he expected me to say, and not having enough energy for it to satisfy him. My marriage was at DefCon one, and even that light was blinking, so I had gotten the impression throughout the afternoon, that he was there to help me salvage it. He didn't hesitate to mention that if there was anything I wanted to talk about, it would stay between us. I knew what he was doing, but he didn't know me well enough to know that it wasn't going to happen.

Along with the fantasy that he could transform an impending divorce into a thriving marriage, Jeff expected me to want a ten-man plumbing operation, replete with trucks, and a building. I could have given him that image, let him pass on a little marriage advice, and allow him to feel good about himself, but I had a good buzz and I had no interest in entertaining any of that. I turned my head to find him staring at me like he was preparing for me to unload my burden. I smirked at the thought and returned my attention to the stars.

I told him I wanted to be anywhere but here. I quickly revised that comment and said I wanted to be on a tropical island with my own tiki bar in a tourist town. People lined up for little umbrella drinks, white sand, and palm trees. My dream is to carve out a piece of the tropics and make it home.

All of this I had kept hidden for a long time, but it was fun to voice it, even if it was only to get a rise out of the guy I was talking to. After five or six glasses of cheap bourbon, his commentary was what I expected, yet no less sobering.

"Wow, that's out there. You come up with some shit, man. But seriously, what about the plumbing business, that's what I mean? Where do you see yourself there in ten years? Something based in reality I hope."

"I don't, or at least I don't want to. You have to understand. I want to be someplace else, thinking about anything other than this. What I told you is the radical change in life that I want someday. The chance to do something unexpected, a chance to do more than just wish I had. That seems real enough." I said.

"Yeah, and whether you like it or not, this is your reality, your life. How come you don't ever talk about owning your own plumb-ing company someday? Hell, you could do that in less than ten years. What you said doesn't make sense." He spoke in low tones, and I could see he was being sincere.

My own plumbing company? I don't think Jeff understood what the object of the game was. When he told me what he wanted out of the next decade, it read like a service manual, a numbered sequence of events and lettered bullet points. He didn't seem to comprehend the exercise, which I thought was to want what you want, not what you could reasonably attain.

"Don't you ever want more? Don't you ever feel like there's something greater inside you? Something that could shift your world? A part of you that you haven't even met yet, but you know is there?" I spoke fervently, trying to somehow make him see, to look farther, to understand that life can be more than what you can simply touch in front of you. And should be.

"Shift your world? Meet someone inside of you? I don't get what you're saying, and frankly, I don't want to. We need to take away that bottle man." His face was an unreadable mask, and he looked lost. Whether that was from the direction of this conversation, or the whiskey, I wasn't sure.

"No, listen, it's like…." I stopped suddenly and just stared at him, my words dried up, I couldn't elaborate anymore. The look on his face told me there was no point.

"You know what your problem is." He finally said.

When he's drunk, he speaks his mind without shame and apologizes the next day.

"No Jeff, what is my problem."

"Forget about what you think is out there, you're not paying enough attention to what's in front of you."

"What does that mean?"

"It means what I said. I hear things. I see what's going on. I thought you'd maybe want to sit here and figure that out. Instead, you're babbling on about something you can never have. You've got to get with the program, man. As I said, what's in front of you needs work, so if you need an ear." He spread his hands to finish his thought.

I couldn't believe what I was hearing, this was a simple end-of-the-night drinking conversation that he had turned personal. Just for the fact that we were two men, and friends, I would have thought he was my ally. But it was starting to feel more like some type of counseling, and he was beginning to piss me off. But I kept it cool, our conversation to this point was measured and thoughtful.

"Look, you asked for my opinion." He said.

"I never asked for your opinion, I told you where I wanted to be in ten years, and you turned it into some kind of a one-man intervention."

"Are you kidding me? I lay out my whole plan for climbing my way to shop foreman and beyond, and you give me this blue-sky bullshit about cocktail lounges in paradise. It's a pipe dream when you can't even take care of here and now." His jabs at my decaying marriage were continuing as if by the mere mention of it we could steer this dialog in its proper direction.

"You think, what, that because our wives are friends, and you seem to have some inside information, that you've got some responsibility to turn this situation around? This is ridiculous. You'll never understand what I want, or what life rattles around in my head if your only goal is to be the shop foreman in some General Motors factory. I feel sorry for you. And by the way, we're not close enough for you to go digging around in my personal life.

"I don't need this shit." He said, shaking his head. "Keep the bottle, I'm going home."

"Good idea."

That's the danger of breaking someone's mold that they've securely placed you in. Funny how you think you know someone, only to discover that you don't. That even though I could practically read his mind in a euchre game, we had nothing else in common. Our relationship, short as it was, dissolved along with my marriage a few months later.

I was mired in the life I had. In the circles I ran in, I met almost no one with much of a passion for anything, let alone a private desire to not just do and be something different but to become the person they were meant to be in the first place, and that's where I was. The reality of my life lay bare before my eyes.

Not horrible, just not what I thought it could be. There were always flickers of what I wanted playing at the fringes of my mind. I knew enough about myself to know I'd never have the courage alone, to step out of one life, and into a completely different world. So, I spent the years working. Finding, strangely enough, an odd peacefulness in it.

## CHAPTER 5

# A new beginning

As spring was pulling itself from the greedy clutches of another long winter, teasing us in the North with glimpses of warmer days that brought thoughts of summer, my ordinary life was about to undergo its own renewal. Our company was part of an annual trade show that took place in March, on the campus of Michigan State University. We were expected to work the entire weekend and Tim had drawn up a schedule on a whiteboard for this two-day event.

"Just so there's no confusion," he said, as he wheeled it out of his office, and parked it where it would be a constant reminder.

Our charge was to take six-hour time blocks and turn ourselves into salesmen. On display was an assortment of all the latest in sparkling plumbing fixtures to upgrade and update your home. Gleaming kitchen and bathroom faucets, white porcelain sinks and toilets, polished water heaters, and an array of things you didn't even know you needed, all basking in the harsh glare of overhead spotlights. With our company name and logo making up the backdrop in reds and blues, it was a bit garish, but at least it wasn't going to be missed.

It was St. Patrick's Day, 2011, and the night the Spartans were playing their first game in the NCAA tournament. The weekend was already penciled in for some overtime with the trade show, so I was looking forward to these couple of days when I could clock out early and watch basketball. My thoughts were broken by the bleating of the two-way radio. Tim tells me that he's somehow missed a work order, a sink that's not draining, and follows up with instructions to turn in the direction of a neighboring town. He sends the address in a text.

The week, to this point, had already been long, filled with its own challenges, and I was tired. My mind had begun its process of laying out the night ahead. I was looking forward to getting home and turning the game on. I had a high-calorie, high-fat game menu to prepare, and snacks to create. It was shaping up to be a fully loaded, one-man buffet of dietary debauchery. After being tugged violently from images of four-cheese nachos, spicy wings, pigs-in-a-blanket, and whatever I could put in my fryer, I replied fictitiously that I was happy to do it. He said it shouldn't be any big deal, and I wondered how he could possibly know that or if he cared that he had just jinxed the whole job.

I've spent enough time watching for the cable guy or waiting for a service call of some kind to know that when they finally get there, I don't expect them to drag their problems or complaints through the door with them. I have the same philosophy when the tables are turned, and instead of waiting, I'm the one providing the service. I've learned over the years that whether my after-work plans were broken by a late service call, or my wife hadn't come home for three days, it doesn't involve my job.

Most of the customers I work for are good people, but they've called because they have a problem, they don't need to add mine to the mix. However, my method of hiding my true sentiments from the customer didn't eliminate those feelings of angst toward my boss, who had waited until my shift was finished to add "one more" service call at the end of an already exhausting day.

I was still giving the windshield a vulgar and uncensored version of my sense of outrage as I slipped off the highway and parked along the exit ramp that leads to the small town of Laingsburg, Michigan. I called the number I was given to alert the customer of my near arrival. I had been in that neighborhood on several occasions, so knowing the general age bracket of its residences, I expected someone a little more elderly to answer. I was caught off guard as a young woman's voice was suddenly in my ear, making her greeting. She said her name was Sheri.

A short pause later I made my introduction, and she proceeded with some idle chit-chat. She knew my boss and was apologizing that I had to come out so late, even though she had called first thing in the morning. I told her it was no problem, I'm happy to do it. Lies. But now I was intrigued by the voice. I've called thousands of people; I've never been distracted by a voice.

I stifled a groan when she said that she was all the way over in Lansing, and it would take her about an hour to get back home. She quickly added that her brother was there, and would I mind if she wasn't home right away. There was an emphasis, and it landed on the word brother when she spoke like she wanted me to know that the guy I was meeting was her flesh and blood, not her husband. I wasn't certain that it actually meant that, in fact, I'm sure it was my imagination. Outside of porn movies, nobody hits on the plumber.

The address led me to a modest walk-out ranch on half an acre in a subdivision that snakes around a large lake just outside of the small town. From the top of the driveway, I could see a patchwork of gardens that were awaiting the coming season, dotting the sloping landscape down to an empty boat dock at the bottom of the back-yard. The view was tranquil, with two white swans cutting a track across the placid water. It put my mind in a good place.

I rang the bell and a man I assume to be Sheri's brother opens the door. He looks to be about ten years older than me with thick, salt and pepper curly hair, and a wild, gnarly beard of the same color. He's dressed head to toe in Mountain Hardware. Later, he confirmed that his socks and shoes were also of that brand. I had never met someone so readily coordinated for camping.

I introduced myself and told him why I'm there, and he said his name is Will, Sheri's brother. I glanced at him, thinking he was coached because I had just heard that same phrase on the phone a few minutes ago. I dismissed the thought as weird, because the way he said it, he seemed to be just giving me information, something that was part of the mantra of his greeting. We face off for a couple of seconds, and I ask him if I should come in before he finally leads me through the door.

The job turned out to be more than I was prepared to handle, and the more I got into it, the worse it got, but Will was fascinating to talk to. While I was trying to unplug the drain, even over the drone of the machine, he went on about his past work experiences, the time he lived in Baltimore, and what happened up in Wisconsin. He didn't seem to leave out the firings, or the failures either, and I liked him for it. He followed me out to my truck to have a look inside. I didn't know he was there, just a voice that appeared behind me with a question, and scared the shit out of me.

"What kind of stuff do you carry in there?"

"What the hell, man, don't sneak up on me like that," I said, after a quick recovery.

"Oh, sorry. What kind of stuff do you carry in there?" He repeated.

"Everything I need to fix just about every plumbing problem, I guess," I answered.

"Oh, it looks pretty organized. Do you ever camp in there?"

"No, I guess I haven't tried that yet. I did accidentally go off-roading once." He didn't seem to get the joke.

"Oh, this one time in Baltimore, when I worked at Home Depot, I tried to get into the plumbing department, but I got fired before I could."

"That's a bummer, what happened?" I asked.

"It was really stupid because I was cooking sausages on the grill in front of the store, and this other guy who worked there told me to move some carts out of the parking lot, and when I was out there the whole grill caught on fire."

"Wow."

"Yeah, they fired me even though it was the other guy's fault. I told them he sent me for carts, but they said I should have been watching the grill."

I wasn't sure how to reply to that, and by good fortune, I didn't have to, because Sheri was just arriving. Will shuffled inside, and Sheri and I chatted for a few minutes in the driveway, it was a nice late afternoon for March in Michigan. I told her that her brother seemed pretty cool and that I liked him. I may have looked like I had a few unspoken questions about him that were certainly none of my business. But as Sheri and I spoke for only ten minutes, it was like we were old friends reunited. At least that was the feeling, later Sheri confirmed that it was hers too.

She tried to play it off like it was no big deal, but I could see it somewhat troubled her; the responsibility of taking care of and watching out for her older brother while trying to balance the rest of her life. In what turned out at the time to be a shortened version, she told me a little about Will.

She said her brother has always been curious about different things, he loved to cook, and he loved creating home remedies and other things that she didn't elaborate on at that time. He experimented, smoked, and dabbled in plants and herbs, and whatever else interested him, and not always for his good. There have been a lot of health issues, she said, and after his breakdown in Wisconsin I've had to worry about him too much over the years, so I decided a while back that he should just live with me. I could see there was tremendous love for her brother, and she showed no embarrassment for his condition, or for what he may have said to me.

We walked inside and I went back to my machine, determined to finish the job, and not entirely certain that I could, only now I had a fresh outlook on the battle. I worked on it for another hour, before finally conceding, and throwing in the towel. I hate leaving a job unfinished, it doesn't fit my vocabulary. But it does happen. I just didn't want it to happen today. I asked Will where Sheri had disappeared to, he said he didn't know and turned back to his coffee.

I dragged the machine out to my truck and met Sheri in the driveway. I apologized and told her there was no way I was getting that drain open. So, as embarrassing as it was to turn a job over to someone else, I gave her the number of a company with a water jet. We talked a little while longer, and I could have sworn there was electricity in the air, as if a thunderstorm were nearby. Will stepped out on the porch and I said goodbye to both of them, leaving their house kicking myself for not at least asking her if I could call sometime.

In all my years in the plumbing business, I have never been attracted to a customer, and I certainly never asked one for a date. It's not who I am. It's unprofessional, and it crosses a boundary that may seem trivial to some, but not to me. It's a tenet that goes far beyond the simple fear of being fired, or slapped.

Although I had been married before, I still had no idea where, and how to meet someone. All of my usual haunts; the bowling alley, the golf course, or the Legion Hall, were unwilling to provide any prospects. Nor did I expect them to. My life at that time was generally work and home. So, I did something for the first time. Well, I sort of half did it.

On the way back to my shop, I picked up my cell phone and called her again. To my surprise, she answered on the first ring. I thought if I was lucky, I might leave her a message, which I was formulating when she was suddenly saying hello. I was caught speechless so I just started babbling.

"Oh, hey! I mean hi, sorry, this is Dave again."

"Yes, I know, I saw the number." She said.

"Um, aah, I was thinking that if you have time tomorrow, I could come back with a bigger machine and give it another try. If you want, I mean. Or you can call the other number I gave you, but I don't mind coming back, or whatever." I thought I sounded pretty confident.

"Okay, Yeah, sound's good, I'll be home around three-thirty, or if you need to come earlier, Will is always there, I mean if you can't come that late." Was there hope in her voice? I thought, maybe.

"No, no, I can come later." Having no idea if my schedule even had an opening for the next day. "Three-thirty I mean, if that's still okay?" Idiot, she just said it was fine.

"Okay, I'll see you then. If you get there early, my brother will be there. Anything else?" she lightly asked.

Are you kidding, how about a chance to know you, to know your family, and your friends? Tell me what kind of life you want, what books you read, what you like to cook. What is it about you that rushes to Wisconsin, or opens your home to your brother because he needs you when most of the people I've met only talk about what they should do? I felt a connection that I hadn't felt in a long time, if ever. But of course, I couldn't say all that.

"No, I guess not, I'll see you tomorrow and I'll get that thing fixed." I hung up.

When we first met in the driveway, she told me how happy she was that I could come that day, because she was having a few of the neighbors over for an Irish dinner to celebrate the holiday, and needed the sink. Now that I had failed in that endeavor, I felt a little guilty that she was shuffling things to another house. But I was going back.

I cleared it with my office the next day, and by two o'clock I was driving back to Laingsburg with a renewed spirit and a bigger machine. Any ideas I had previously entertained involving a short work day, and rushing home to watch basketball, had been completely forgotten. A recreant thought crossed my mind, that maybe she'd turn this around, and ask me if I wouldn't mind a phone call. It's never happened before, but who knows?

I was in a heavyweight battle with my own personal code, and it had me on the ropes. After all, if I was reading this wrong, then I'd be sacrificing one of my few principles only to look like some kind of a creep. I felt like I was crazy. I had a job to do, yet I was filled with adolescent hormones affecting all manner of thinking. My mind, normally sound, was spinning its own interpretations of the day before. It doesn't stand to reason otherwise.

When I got there, Will was waiting for me at the door and asked me if I wanted a cup of coffee. I said sure, and he showed me where the cups were, and pointed out the coffee pot. After pouring myself a cup I tried making conversation, asking him mundane questions that were overlooked during our initial meeting. He was withdrawn and didn't seem to have much to say, so I told him I'd better get to work, and went outside to collect the stuff I needed.

About an hour into the nightmare, Sheri came home, and I was no closer to getting the problem solved than when I had left the day before. I told her Will and I were getting pretty irritated about it. She looked over at Will, serene as an angel, and laughed. And all my anger was swept away.

We talked while I worked for the next hour before I finally surrendered. Again. I had it draining a little, but even that wasn't going to last. It should get you through the weekend I said, but you'll need to call the guy with the water jet next week. I led her to the basement and pointed out all the twists and turns, and obvious problems with the drain as it meandered its way across the ceiling above, before finally ending at the main sewer. All very exciting, I'm sure.

I was reaching for whatever I could to keep her talking. I wasn't very good at this, I knew. To my credit, she seemed thoroughly impressed, and that bewildered look only meant she was deep in thought on what I had just told her. I don't always read women very well. We went upstairs to the kitchen, and I gathered up my tarps and tools.

The small talk concerning the dinner, the neighbors, and the weather, since arriving at the door to my truck, was stretching to uncomfortable lengths and had essentially run out of steam. I didn't think I would say anything. But in the seconds that I stood there debating with myself, it just popped out. I ended the argument when I decided not to look back someday and wonder, so I asked her if she'd wanna do something, sometime. She said I'd love to, when. I said I'd give her a call. She seemed satisfied.

The following day was taken up working the company booth at the trade show. It's not how I recommend allowing a beautiful Saturday to go by, locked in a convention hall, but I had no choice. I managed to fill the time I wasn't chained to someone, talking about their plumbing, by poking Sheri's number into my phone and giving up before hitting the last digit. It must have been entertaining because I did it all day.

Throughout that endless afternoon, I pulled my phone out at least a dozen times, only to put it away again. I can assure you that I know nothing of the rules of engagement here. When was too soon to call? How much time passes before it becomes too late? Are less than twenty-four hours acceptable for either? I didn't know, and I didn't care.

When I got to my car it was four o'clock and I had thought about this long enough. Despite my fears of coming off a little desperate, which I wasn't, just overcome, I finally let the call go through. She picked up on the third ring and had to say hello twice before I began stammering.

"Oh, hey, uh this is Dave, you know, from your house, the plumber?" I sound like Don Juan.

"I didn't think anyone was there, hello Dave the plumber. I didn't expect you to call so soon." She said.

Shit, I knew I'd get the timing wrong.

"I'm sorry, is this a bad time? I can call back later, or another time, or not at all, whatever you want. I hope this is okay?" I was trying to be cool, and instead, I was tripping all over myself.

"No, no, it's fine, how's it going? I mean, what are you doing?" She replied.

"I just finished working the trade show out here on the east side and I thought, I don't know, maybe we could hang out if you want. The Pub in Laingsburg has a nice happy hour. Or if you're busy it's no problem. Or if you don't want to." I said.

"Well, I'm cooking dinner for Will right now, he wants to eat early and I'm not hungry, plus he's a vegetarian so I'm trying to come up with something new."

"Okay, sounds like fun." And I meant it, I love to cook. "We can try another time; sorry I surprised you so soon."

"No, no, why don't you come over here at like six, I've got some beer in the fridge. We don't need to go anywhere; we can sit on the patio and look out at the lake. Way less noise anyway, if you want." It sounded like the only thing I wanted.

"Yeah, sounds great, Okay I'll see you then." And I hung up.

I managed to kill the longest two hours of my life, picked up a six-pack of Corona, and showed up a little after six. I didn't want it to look like I was waiting around the corner, which of course, I was.

The back and forth between us seemed to come so easy, sharing so much in common, that it couldn't be real. But it was. We settled into conversation like we'd done it a hundred times, and flowed seamlessly from one topic to the next. Food, cooking, grilling, summers on the lake, her neighbors, our jobs, our lives. It was amazing how everything just seemed to click into place. At one point, into our second beer, and after I had mentioned that I was a fan of Civil War history, she asked me.

"Have you ever read The Killer Angels? About the battle of Gettysburg?"

"What, do you mean by Michael Shaara? I've worn-out two copies, It's fantastic writing, so alive." I glanced over with a look of surprise.

"How did you ever come upon that book?"

"Someone left it in our office, so I thought I'd give it a read and I loved it, couldn't put it down." She said.

"I know, right, I love the beginning, only one man, the spy, knows the position of both armies as they approach Gettysburg. Chamberlain defending Little Round Top, the peach orchard, Pickett's insane charge. Sorry." I looked away in embarrassment. "I've already said this but, I can't believe we've read the same book and loved it, especially one that's not necessarily mainstream. Did you read the other two?" I quickly added.

"No, what other two? I didn't know he wrote more."

"He did, but not about that. It's his son. You've got to read the other two." I get passionate about books and history, and a little of that was showing now.

"What do you mean, his son? She said, confused.

"His son Jeff wrote two books that perfectly bookend The Killer Angels, the guy is brilliant. What he created was a saga that put his father's book in the middle. Together they detail the entire conflict, from Sumpter to Appomattox. His words and descriptions are so alive, that you become a part of the story.

"Wow, his writing touched you somehow, I can see it. I'll look on E-bay."

"Don't bother, I have them. I mean, not with me now, at my house, I'll give them to you." I said.

On it went like that into the evening, just sitting on her back deck nursing a couple of beers, relating stories, and feeling more vital than I had in a long time. We were just two people wandering through life, thrown together late by a chance meeting, a random collision of worlds, who it seemed may have found something worth holding on to.

I told her I should probably get going, it was getting late and I had to work the trade show again the next day, so we went inside to say goodbye. Emotions were stirring in me that had lain dormant for too long. To completely connect with someone so suddenly was a little startling. It took me by surprise. She took me by surprise.

First dates like this, if that's what you'd call it, at any age can be awkward at best. Feeling your way around each other's history, likes, dislikes, friends, family, and everything else that goes into our make-up is exhausting. But this wasn't like that, not even close. It was as if we already knew each other. That's an exaggeration of course, but that was the feeling.

Once inside, I took a quick look around the kitchen, my eyes passing over the sink that through the last two days had given me so much grief, and at the same time brought me so much joy, before finally realizing that her brother was missing.

"Where's Will been?"

"I asked him to stay downstairs and watch a movie so we could talk alone." She said.

"Oh, I'm sorry, you didn't have to do that, I like Will."

"Thank you for liking him, and yes I did, otherwise he'll be asking you questions all night, and talking about Baltimore."

"He mentioned Baltimore earlier," I said.

"He'll mention more, anyway I didn't want that. Besides, he's always here, you'll see him plenty." That last line made me smile.

"Okay, tell him I'll see him again, I guess, and you too, I hope."

"You will, what are you doing Friday night, next week."

"I have nothing going on, ever really," I said, sheepishly.

"Come over, we can take a walk and I'll show you the park. Molly loves to run and chase tennis balls into the water. It'll be fun." She pleaded.

Molly was her beautiful black lab who, after our initial meeting and hello's, mostly just lounged in the corner of the kitchen, skeptical and uninterested.

"It does sound like fun. After work, say five or six?"

"Perfect, I'll make dinner." She said.

"Okay, then I guess I'll see you Friday, and don't be surprised if I call you before that.

"I hope so."

Not knowing what else to do, I gave her a quick hug and went out the door to my car. I know, pretty lame, but as I reached for my door handle, I heard her call out behind me.

"Hey mister, I think you forgot something."

I turned around still smiling, and she met me with a kiss. Although momentarily surprised, I kissed her back. And in that kiss, I saw every dream I ever had. In that moment everything was possible, and yet nothing mattered, I had found what was missing in my life.

Warmth spread through me on that chilly March night as we separated. I just stared into those blue eyes and saw forever. I think at that moment we both knew that we might have discovered something unique and potentially valuable, something desperately needed, but still fragile. More than just falling in love, but kindling an easy-going, deep friendship. There were sure to be some obstacles ahead, but we weren't lost anymore.

## CHAPTER 6

# A view to the future

Almost a year from the day we met, Sheri and I found ourselves touching down on the island of Kauai after leaving snowy Detroit the night before. It was, and still is, the most enchanted and beautiful place I have ever been. Two, or three months before, Sheri floated the idea of going to Hawaii to see if I had any interest. I did. I knew that she and her ex-husband owned a condo on the island that was still unresolved, two years after the divorce. His determined overvaluing of the property made it impossible to sell, so it was left as a vacation rental where it broke even.

I saw no reason to get into the middle of that tricky situation, and Sheri agreed. So, we avoided any potential hassles, and from my experience with the man, there would have been many, and elected instead, to lease a little place overlooking the ocean. From her online search of places to stay on the island, Sheri found us the perfect spot.

Within the course of our ten-day trip, the island of Kauai showed us just how magnificent she is. No open road was left untouched by us, as we explored every mile in wonder. The Island had its own mystery about it. As if it would continue to reveal itself, no matter how long you lived there. What was difficult to explain to Sheri at the time was the feeling I had of coming home, of finding home. I don't know how, but I knew the second I got off that plane, that we would someday live there. I had found where I belonged.

As we moved through the days on that first trip, we drove everywhere, seeking every corner we could find. I think I could see her coming around to what I was feeling, to the idea that we don't have to be locked into the life we've set for ourselves. I mean, if paradise is what we're looking for, this is it. Let's figure out how to live here, how to open a tiki bar, or a restaurant, or something.

These thoughts were running around in my head, with no inkling on how to get there, or to a greater extent, where to begin, but it was possible, that I definitely knew. We were smart and tenacious, and I felt we could take on any vision. I only hoped that Sheri could see this one, because although we had discussed the idea of a restaurant before, throughout the previous year, the shape, in my mind, was becoming altogether different.

Then I would glance over from the driver's seat and catch a certain look on her face, charmed and captivated, and I could tell the wheels were turning. And I knew we were on the same page. Even though she had been to Kauai on several occasions, I think in her own way she was seeing it for the first time, or at least from a new perspective.

Let me go back and tell you what led to these compelling and persuasive thoughts, and the idea that we might entertain another life. Through that first spring and summer together, Sheri and I were inseparable. We'd meet up for lunch, or dinner, catch a movie, or just jump in her convertible and drive. More than once we threw the top down on a perfect weekend and found ourselves in Chicago, where Sheri grew up and still has family.

I introduced myself to Lee, Sheri's youngest brother, on a warm Friday afternoon in late May. He had driven up from the windy city for the long weekend to help put the boat in the water and officially kick off the summer. Sheri and I had just started dating in March and she'd been wanting me to meet him almost from the start. With both of their parents gone, Lee and Will were the only close family she had left.

Foregoing the mail and the still waiting spring yard work at my house, I went straight to her place from my final call. Knowing there was no chance I would see my own house that weekend, I threw some things in a travel bag before I left for work and grabbed an extra cooler.

Her two brothers had everything set by the time I got there, so we started unloading beer and ice from the back of my van, and packing them in the coolers for a quiet little cruise out on the water. The boys were standing outside drinking Old Style, and smoking Camels when I pulled up, so I knew immediately that we would get along just fine, and we did. After introductions, handshaking, and filling the coolers, I joined them in a beer and a smoke and we started asking each other questions and telling stories.

Sheri was apparently inside making snacks and popped out the door a few minutes later to see if I had gotten there yet. The look on her face was priceless like she couldn't comprehend what she was seeing. Three guys in her driveway, holding beers and laughing like idiots. It took her a second, and then she joined in while walking over to put her arm around me. And my heart melted.

"Well, I see you two have already met." She said.

"Yes, yes we have," I said, trying to stop laughing.

"What's so funny anyway." She said, pushing Lee in the chest with her hand.

"I don't know, Will said something that just caught us both wrong I guess, he's worried about the boat, you know, first time out and all. I mean that's not what got us laughing, I'm just saying." Lee replied.

"Well, anyway Lee, this is Dave." She drew the two names out slowly.

"Hello! We've been standing here fifteen minutes filling coolers, what, you think we haven't met yet." Said Lee, laughing.

"Well, hell, I don't know, I just walked out here.

Aah, the banter of brother and sister.

I threw out my hand and said, hey Lee I'm Dave, and for some reason, that was enough to get us going again. She waved her arms in mock exasperation as she slowly disappeared into the house, a smile on her face the whole time, knowing that I was accepted by the two people that mattered the most to her. I knew it was important to her, as I guess it would be to most people, that Lee and I would hit it off, and would, to her great delight, become friends. Which, going on eleven, almost twelve years now, is exactly what happened.

When Sheri came out the door with enough stuffed mushrooms, shrimp dip, and corn salsa to feed the block, we quickly jumped in to help her and carried everything across the backyard and onto the boat. Dock lines were cast off, and the motor caught on the second try, and with a neat one-eighty, Lee had us pointing toward the outlet of the small channel.

"We're meeting Harley and Brenda on the back lake, and Kelli's picking up Eric at his dock. I'm sure everyone else will be out there." She said, as Lee edged up the throttle for the literal two-minute cruise to the back of the lake, where there were no houses to be bothered by the noise.

It was the beginning of our quest to make great food. Blending flavors, and combinations of ingredients that would find a home together. We spent much of our free time exploring ideas and discovering spices, marrying and creating recipes that were uniquely our own. I love to put together marinades, rubs, and sauces, and I can cook, grill, smoke, or sauté anything that once swam, flew, grazed in a pasture, or grew in a field. Sheri however, has this amazing ability to take bits and pieces, and elements of several recipes, including family, and join them together to create something that borders on magical.

It seemed like every other weekend we were cooking and preparing something new, then trying it out on our neighbors in small bites. It was a good feeling to load up the boat with whatever we had made and cruise the lake handing out samples to anyone we encountered, while we accosted our friends dock to dock.

Whether it was three different styles of pork sandwiches on three different buns, grilled portabellas topped with provolone, basil, and balsamic, or ceviche tacos with fresh Pico de Gallo from our garden, we were putting together some good flavors. We were consumed, not in the fine art of cooking, but the lost art of great cooking. We spent so many of our weekends making drinks, creating appetizers, and entertaining neighbors that we began to build a real passion for it. It was a role I could see myself fitting into somewhere in the future.

The majority of that splendid season known as summer, which I had only then re-discovered, was undeniably spent on the lake, or in it, with a packed cooler and plenty of food. Like everywhere we touch, the memories we forged on that small piece of water will stay with us forever. Scenic Lake was a wonderful party host, bringing together neighbors, friends, new acquaintances, and a lot of laughter, till well into the night.

The girl beside me was becoming everything to me, and I knew I loved her. We had so much more than simple life connections in common. We shared the same ideas, thoughts, beliefs, and surprisingly, the same dreams. It wasn't just our hearts that began to merge as one, however. More and more of my stuff was ending up in her garage.

Since Sheri and I lived about forty-five minutes apart, I was seeing less and less of my house that summer and it showed. I allowed minimal time to pick up the mail and cut the grass, and by the time I noticed the bushes and beds in the back, I had already lost interest. They were on their own and running wild. It seemed inevitable that we would share the rest of our lives together, and what better place than on the lake, so I finally sold my house and moved to Laingsburg.

In July of that summer, Sheri had planned a trip to Texas to visit a couple of friends she hadn't seen in a while. The getaway to their Galveston home was conceived before we met, and when she updated them on her personal life, they demanded that she bring me along. Any awkwardness that I anticipated was put immediately to bed at the introduction of these people. Their love for Sheri was evident, but the genuine warmth they showed me went well beyond the meeting of strangers.

They said that in a few days when we had adjusted more to the climate, they had an exciting excursion arranged. It was so unbearably hot, that I couldn't imagine how anyone could adjust to this. I only hoped the excursion included air conditioning. The temperature was passing through the upper nineties and still climbing. A swim in the Gulf gave no relief, so we stayed inside mostly, where the air was cooler. I couldn't figure out how anyone could live here, every breath I took was so laden with humidity, that the need to wring out my lungs had crossed my mind more than once.

The large fishing boat that Andy and Donna owned was moored in a slip a few miles down the Texas coast. One morning, before the sun came up, and at an hour I didn't recognize, we found ourselves tumbling from the backseat of a Ford quad-cab, and landing in the dimly lit parking lot of a quiet marina. When we arrived at the dock, the four huge Mercury outboards were already vigorously bubbling the water at the stern, as if they could hardly contain themselves, anxious to do their work.

A rough and pebbled fiberglass deck, that encircled the pilot-house, met our feet and ensured there would be no slipping while pulling in the big one, and padded benches marked out the obvious seating areas. I thought the steel tubes that were mounted along the railings were for holding bottles of rum, or pirate flags, but as Andy started dropping long fishing poles into them, I discovered that it was nothing quite so exotic.

We motored and bounced our way out into the Gulf of Mexico until I lost sight of land. Which is awesome if you're on a cruise ship, with a drink in hand looking for the pool. It's a little unsettling in a forty-foot fishing boat, bucking in all directions like your worst day at the rodeo. Also, as the sun set its track and advanced along that line, I discovered there was no air-conditioning. We fished all day. I remembered too late that I didn't like fishing. It was monotonous. You never stop rolling up and down, and there was no escape from the sun. Cast after cast I reeled in red snapper that were too small, only to throw them back. I didn't get the thrill.

"Isn't this fun, I could do this all day, and be just fine," Andy said to me.

As the day progressed, he had run a continuous litany on the art and craft of open sea fishing, and I could see that this man was living his dream. He explained lures and barbs and what we would bait them with. He described spoons, spinners, and swivels, how the reel operated, and where to stand on the boat. He went over how the live well worked, how to cast, and the importance of making sure the lines don't cross and tangle. I poked a small squid onto the hook I was supplied with and was instantly rewarded with a squirt of black ink across my shorts. He reminded me to watch out for that too.

We caught enough mahi, king mackerel, and red snapper to feed us for a couple of days, and we finally eased our way back to shore on what seemed the longest day of my life. I could see Sheri was in the same condition. From our outward appearance, of course, our wonderful hosts knew none of this. We were sincerely appreciative of the experience, and a good day shared. I just know that I would never charter a fishing boat. Ever.

That night, their two sons and their wives joined us, and we all pitched in for a delicious dinner from what we had just caught. Pan-fried snapper, grilled mahi-mahi, fish dip, and steamed mackerel. We threw together a large kale and walnut salad with a zesty vinaigrette, and cut up some fresh fruit from the farmers market. We sat down to a couple of bottles of cold chardonnay and offered a toast to love, life, and happiness. The food, the conversation, the wine, it was perfect.

That image was a snapshot of what I felt life, boiled down, should be about. The gathering of friends and family, strangers who become friends, and an atmosphere of warmth and togetherness.

Later that night, after everything was cleaned up and we were finishing the last of the wine, Sheri and I sat on the porch facing the Gulf alone, and simply took it in. We were exhausted, the 4 a.m. wake-up call, the day on the water, the sun, fishing, and the food, they had all taken their toll.

The stars were tiny points in the sky, shining bright in the absence of the moon. The breeze was tinged with the smell of salt, and sea. The wind sweeping through the palms and the waves crashing on the beach were the only sounds, and I thought I could live with that for the rest of my life. As we lounged in the open air on a second-floor deck in Galveston, Texas, looking out at the blackness that would be the shimmering Gulf of Mexico in the light of day, we quietly let our minds wander.

"Wouldn't it be cool to own a place with the kind of feel we just experienced tonight," Sheri said, breaking the silence.

"Um, yeah. What do you mean?"

"Well, if we took our lives in another direction like we've brought up before. I mean, we both ultimately want something different right? Then I could see us owning some kind of restaurant, or a bar, or something between the two, I don't know, but I want the atmosphere of tonight to be a huge part of it. Great food, great friends, sort of a coming-together feel, like family. Am I making any sense?"

"You're making perfect sense, that's exactly what I want too. If we can do it where the palm trees are visible, I'm in. I'm just not sure how to get there." I said, surprised.

"I don't know either, but we'll figure it out, once we decide what it is we really want and how we want to spend the rest of our lives."

"Yeah, I get it. This has been good though, this trip. I feel like we both want the same things. You know, together we can do about anything we want, wherever we want. What about Texas?" I said.

"I think I'd suffocate down here. Besides, there's so much open space." She seemed doubtful.

"Yeah, it does have its extremes. It's pretty though. I guess the northern part of the state might be cooler, I don't know, but then you lose the palms. I don't feel any pull to be here, nothing against Texas, I just don't think I want to live here. There's no, what, harmony I guess is the only word I can think of, but who knows, things change..." I trailed off and we sat in silence once again.

"I feel the same way that you do." Her sudden words startled me. I think I was drifting off.

"What?"

"You said you didn't feel any kind of pull, like a need to be here, and I feel the same way. I'm not sure if harmony is the right word for it though, but it's close." She went silent.

"Yeah, we'll figure it out."

The next afternoon we walked back from the beach, panting like dogs from the humidity, and tried to cool off with a shower. It didn't work, so we did the next best thing and started drinking. Sheri was squeezing fresh grapefruit through a strainer and mixing it with tequila, triple sec, and lime juice.

If we take three fingers of good whiskey out of the equation, then she had just created the best drink I've ever had. The grapefruit margarita. A tart and tangy mix with a touch of sweetness and copious amounts of Don Julio, all swimming together under a lightly salted rim. It woke up the senses and the afternoon turned into our own little happy hour. It was perfect. The air conditioner was struggling to keep up, but after mixing our third tall glass, they were both doing their job and I was feeling pretty good. I couldn't be happier, or more at peace with myself, as we stood in that kitchen drinking margaritas and just beginning to point our eyes to the future.

"You know these are going on our menu someday." I said with a wink.

"You're damn right." She said smiling.

It was a turning point in our lives. We came home from Texas with a solid idea of what we wanted our future to look like. If we didn't know where we wanted to be, at least we knew what we ultimately wanted to become. Although dedicated and quite effective in what we did for a living, we were both, nonetheless, disenchanted with the future of our chosen careers and in my case, the career itself. We were drawn together, and while that was enough, we knew we could do so much more than simply plan for retirement.

Sheri was a health insurance agent for a local firm, guiding her clients through a shrinking market to find the plan that best fit their employees and their budget, and usually not in that order. Super boring. I mean it paid well enough, but I could see that all the continuous changes and the monotony of endless paperwork was not where she saw herself in ten years. No idle desk job, no matter how important, or how high up the ladder, could ever captivate her imagination, or even begin to stimulate her brain.

The more we got to know each other, the more I discovered the amazing, creative mind inside the woman who stole my heart. Something alive and crazy, and all at once special, resides inside her and demands that she think beyond the borders of reason. Her brain is always exploring and processing the 'what-ifs', looking closely at the angles that others only see as impossible.

As time continued at its usual pace, summer rolled into winter, and Sheri, Will, and I were adapting to a new life, and doing a pretty good job of it, even Molly seemed to accept that I wasn't going anywhere. As long as I threw her the tennis ball, or reached for the bag of bacon strips we were like best friends. Dogs.

Will and I were getting closer, and a level of comfort had grown between us almost to the point of brotherhood. I'd collect him from his spot at the dining room table, and enlist his help in a few projects I had going here and there outside. It turned out that he specialized in drinking coffee and smoking while I worked, but it was good company. We'd pass the time talking about whatever came up and discovering more about each other than we knew the day before. Eventually, the project seemed to finish itself.

We've had a lot of conversations together about life, history, work, and other things. Sometimes while drinking around a campfire, Will would share his ideas about the lost city of Atlantis, or outline his theory on angels, going deep into each subject. Later I would ask Sheri to translate a few things that I didn't understand, because she knew him so well, knew the details of his life so well. And she would, without malice for either of us. He's unique among most people I know. A quiet, gentle soul, with a rarely seen streak of mischief.

Although Sheri grew up with five brothers, the age differences spanned more than twenty years, so she was always closest to Lee and Will, one slightly younger, one slightly older. As a consequence of this trinity, I grew closer to them as well. We spent a lot of time together. The four of us would head off somewhere camping, skiing, or meet for long weekends along the Lake Michigan shore in small towns like Saugatuck, or South Haven. Like my sister and I, she had very little contact with the others, possibly for much the same reasons, or at least close enough to be interchangeable, so I've never pressed the issue, nor have I ever met them.

We had entered a new chapter in our lives. One that hinted, on that small lake in Laingsburg, Michigan, to a different future than we had ever imagined. When Sheri and I first got together, we knew we had found something special, an end to a search that we didn't even know we were making. So, when we blended our separate lives into one, without adding any extra debt, or unnecessary baggage, it just worked, and it felt right. We began to put our ideas on paper, filling page after page with our thoughts, recipes, crudely drawn sketches, and calculations for what we ultimately wanted. At times it read like the manifesto of a madman, but once decoded it held the roadmap of where our life would go.

## CHAPTER 7

# An emotional farewell

A s our bodies flew back to Michigan, our hearts were forever lost
to Kauai. I couldn't put into words how I was feeling on that
first trip, or what kind of switches had been turned on for me. I
spent most of the flight home wrapping my mind around the idea
of a life on that fabulous island and what that would mean. The
change of culture and the adjustment to the tropics, not to mention
an entirely new way of life, were only scratching the surface. There
was the anxiety of uprooting and selling the house, leaving everyone
behind, and the blind faith it would take to run headlong towards
a dream. And let's not forget the money.

There was my mom and Will to think about. I figured Will
would probably go with us, although I wasn't even sure I could
presume that, and I certainly wasn't sure I was ready to just up and
leave my mother behind. So much to consider, so much unsurety.
In the end, after wrestling with these tangled thoughts, it made no
difference. They were just my usual daydreams, the things I mostly
keep locked up in my head. But I must admit, for the first time this
felt different, with a solid plan, it felt possible.

Sheri and I had gone to Kauai for a needed vacation. It was a simple getaway from the monotony of work and a northern winter, and yet completely unexpected, we found the place our future would take us. Early on that first trip, with the setting sun shimmering through the palm trees and falling into the ocean, we were married in a ceremony on our lanai. It was just the two of us, so small the official stood in as the witness, but it was all that we needed. Without any friends or support group, without knowing a single person on the island, Sheri and I, in our own way, discovered home.

Over the next couple of years, we quietly schemed and laid plans that would lead us to our vision of what we wanted. We continued to bombard our friends and neighbors with an array of items from our kitchen. We had lake parties, garage parties, and winter bonfires where we passed around shots of tequila, and dined on lamb tacos. We were always cooking, grilling, or frying something, and our neighbors were always more than happy to be the test market.

It was our travels around Kauai, where we sampled all the flavors of the island, that gave us the idea of mixing a midwestern palate with the taste of the tropics everyone expects to find. We experienced traditional Polynesian means of making and preparing meals. Fish and pork steamed in banana leaves, taro pounded into poi, and whole pigs baked with vegetables in an underground oven called an Imu. It was so different from our own mainland way of doing things that it brought a uniqueness to the entire process.

The ideas and thoughts on our future that Sheri and I were passing back and forth made me want to leave Michigan immediately and throw ourselves into island life. But, there was fear in those thoughts as well. Failure was at the top of the list. And not just failure, but failure so far away. Other concerns crowded our minds along with it. Friends, neighbors, Sheri's family, distance, and, of course, my mom.

It's such a strange, unpredictable world we live in at times. How many times over just the last year, did I argue the case between staying, or chasing my desire? How much time did I waste ruminating back and forth, when all along there was only one thing that held me in place? Long enough to come to the decision that if my mother's health was not well, and it hadn't been for some time, that I wasn't going anywhere. I needed to be there for her, whatever that meant, and Sheri, without flinching, understood that.

Our plans and conceptions for the future would press on, the notebooks and folders would continue to grow, but our passion and desire for another life would wait. My mom was the only cord that kept me bound to the present, rooted to the here and now, and a lifetime of gradual care and maintenance had only served to strengthen it.

On the day before my forty-sixth birthday the bond that I shared with my mother, a link that had been forged through the fire of trial and many errors until it remained strong and resilient through the years, shattered in the wake of a final breath. She passed away in a hospital room about two miles from where I grew up. She was only sixty-seven. I had never told her that I planned someday to move five thousand miles away, that life was sweeping Sheri and I in another direction, and what that direction was. For some reason, even with everything I felt comfortable talking to her about, it never felt right. I wish now I had. I've been through plenty of events in my life but losing my mother was by far the worst.

I had known for years that her unwavering lifestyle and deteriorating condition would eventually shorten her life. After several discussions that degraded into all-out wars about her health and the fact that she was blatantly contributing to its decline, I finally gave up. As much as it hurt me to watch my mom self-destruct before my eyes, I chose to stop being so damn combative and at times self-righteous and just love her, and make sure that she knew that I loved her, because I knew I was never going to change her, and believe me, it was tough. That was a decision some of her closest friends could not come to. They were not able to set aside their own judgment, and in the end, that hurt her more than any physical pain she was going through.

An hour after my father called me with the news that my mother had suffered a heart attack and was fading fast, I was at the hospital holding her hand. When she finally exhaled her last breath later in the day, I had lost not only my mother and a mentor but a truly great friend. Someone I could count on to always listen, not always agree, but always listen. A lifetime of memories flooded back to me as they often do at these times. I left the room on legs I didn't trust and wrapped my arms around my wife. She was crying.

In the days and weeks that followed, I came to realize a simple truth about the relationship I had with my father. A fact that generally stayed hidden in the shadows during the time my mother was alive. It's something I think I've always known but chose to ignore for most of my life. I discovered that now that she was gone, there seemed to be nothing left to hold my father and I together. It's not that we didn't get along. What little I continued to see of him. It's just that we didn't seem to have any interest in keeping company.

Without my mom in the mix, nothing was the same, and there was little to talk about. It became obvious early on that we wouldn't be sharing stories of my mother, or bringing about any closure to the wound that her death had inflicted. She was a topic that for his own reasons he wouldn't broach. We made visits, watched a couple of ballgames, and he called me to take a few plumbing jobs when they wouldn't fit his schedule, but through it all, we drifted a little farther apart.

A few months later, Sheri and I were doing a little sprucing up around the outside of my parents' weekend getaway. Although now, I guess it was just my dad's place. He showed up as we were bagging the last of the plant debris. We were not expecting him so soon and rushed over to greet him with a hug. We had brought with us a beautiful outdoor glider, normally stationed on our front porch, that Sheri thought would look better there. We placed it along a crushed stone path between the shed where the golf cart was stored, and the firepit. The thanks on his face as he surveyed the work we'd done, as a gift from our heart, was evident, but was also overshadowed by a look of uneasy distraction.

I grabbed a bottle of Bad Ass, popped the top, and sat down at the picnic table that over the years has listened in on countless conversations and stories throughout my adult life. It's where we re-hashed the golf scores and counted the cost of decisions made, of mistakes made. It's where my mom and I would criticize the Tigers in late summer for another wasted year, and where my dad and I put together the Weber all those years ago. It's where I sat with my mom and opened my heart. Where I slid the envelope in front of my dad when I passed the state plumbing exam, and knew on that count, that he'd be proud.

He sat down opposite, lighting a cheap smoke that he pulled from an old pack and began to preoccupy himself by picking at the paint flaking off the edge of the table. Since the death of my mother, he has said little, if anything, about her. In fact, he hated talking about her so much that he would quickly change the subject or walk away when anybody brought up a story or anecdote about her. I thought it was part of grief, except while I always tried to keep her memory alive, he affected silence, bordering on disinterest.

"I've been meaning to re-coat this." He said absently.

"It holds a lot of memories." A lead-in to what I finally thought was coming. I waited.

"Well, I guess I've got something to say." Shifting in his seat he was clearly uncomfortable, which I found ironic.

"Okay, shoot," I said.

Sheri was sweeping the brick patio next to us and indicated that she would continue while he spoke. She, like I, assumed he was finally going to open up about my mother, maybe cry, share some emotion or memories, or even defend the way he'd been acting the past few months or so. Hell, maybe his whole life. But no, I couldn't have been more wrong.

"I guess it's time I tell you that I've been seeing a woman for a couple of months now. We decided that she should sell her house and move in with me."

"What?" I said, confused.

I was sitting on the edge of the bench in awkward anticipation of a conversation that to this point, I had never had with my dad, nor ever thought I would. A heart-to-heart, a moment of shared grief. What he said was so unexpected that it sounded like a foreign language. The sweeping stopped.

"Jill is concerned that if something happens to me after she sells her house, you might kick her out, and then she's got nowhere to go since you're willed the house and all."

Forget the fact that I had never heard of this person before. He never once mentioned that he might be interested in someone, or that he was planning to start dating. How did we jump all the way to giving her the house? What the fuck was he talking about?

I couldn't get my head wrapped around the new direction. He had once again pulled the rug out from under me and sent my mind reeling.

"But, what about mom? I thought…" I trailed off in a voice that sounded twelve and in preadolescent emotion. I was thrown a curve ball that seemed to come from Saturn's rings.

"Well…." He shrugged his shoulders as if to say 'what are you going to do.' That simple gesture really pissed me off.

"What you're saying doesn't make any sense. Do you have any idea what you're telling me? My mother, your wife of *forty-nine* years has been gone less than three months, and you have barely had a word to say, never once putting your feelings on display, or at the very least allowing me to share mine. Now you apparently have so little respect for what's left of your family that you think this is suddenly an appropriate conversation? As though it's the next logical event that follows the death of someone you love. What is wrong with you? Who the hell is Jill?" I unknowingly found myself standing now, looking around in confusion as if trying to locate the nearest exit and finding my feet unable to carry me there.

His answer was as indifferent as his attitude. "I have friends that I talk to when I want to. I just don't feel like I need that."

"But I do," I said.

"Then find someone to talk to, because I don't, and in time you won't either. I think you'll like Jill. We have a good time together. I don't want to be alone. It's boring," he said, "besides…I'm just moving on, doing what I think is right for me."

"What you think is right for you? Do you really not have an ounce of thought for anyone but yourself? The fact that we're even having this conversation, involving what, the needs of an unknown woman you've been dating for two months, tells me no. You don't seem capable of showing any emotion, ever, but does that also affect your better judgment?" I was hurt, sad, and angry, running a full gamut of emotions that overtook me in mere seconds, while he just sat there stone-faced and unmoved.

"I don't think this is as big a deal as you're making it out to be." He said.

I couldn't believe what I was hearing, my mother had just died, and for me, those emotions were still raw. I wanted him to be able to move on. To find his own level of comfort and happiness in this sudden and shifting life change. I just assumed he'd do it with some degree of dignity. For a fleeting second, before he started talking, I thought something unheard of was going to take place and we would move towards healing. But no. There would be no heart-to-heart, no tears, no coming together, no healing, only an expanding distance.

I stood there looking at him and slowly shook my head. Sheri had crept up next to me. I was so worked up that I had forgotten she was there, but she was my anchor in all of this. She had no one close to her after her own mother passed away and she made sure it wouldn't be the same for me. I took her hand and felt her love and compassion, and a sudden understanding was dawning.

As I stood there, shocked by the misdirection that this conversation had taken, everything I ever knew about my father blew through me like a December wind. It finally hit me, or maybe I stopped dodging. From the time I was maybe twelve years old, my mother would often tell me not to turn into my father, usually when she was angry, or on the verge of tears. As a teenager, I always thought she meant don't grow up to be a jerk, but I saw it time and time again, as far back as I dared to look. My father cared about no one but himself, and he had proven it over and over.

He dropped the gavel for the final verdict and in that moment, I knew where I belonged. I pitied the man in front of me, he was lately unequal to the task of making a good decision. There had been a string of instances over the past few months that upheld this estimate. My father didn't know me, and worst of all he didn't want to. I found it telling that I had never met this woman. That he had never once mentioned her, and that she didn't insist on joining my dad on this unholy errand and in the process meet his only son and his wife. For me, it spoke volumes about her character. And his for that matter.

My father unfortunately broke the silence with what was obviously the most important thing on his self-absorbed mind.

"Well…It is what it is. So, what about the house?"

The request itself was ridiculous. I mean, was he on his deathbed? I didn't think so. Would the woman in question be around in six months? A year? Maybe. But it still wouldn't merit even the thought of this discussion. Besides, he could change his will any way he wanted. His priorities on what seemed to matter to him were way out of whack and even after all this time, I still couldn't understand his lack of empathy. I said none of those things.

"I'm not interested in your house, so do whatever you want, you seem to excel at that." I found my feet, and my wife along with them, angling toward the car.

"We're moving to Kauai, by the way. I don't know when, but I know it's time. I have nothing holding me here. When I called you to see if you would be here this weekend, we thought it would be a good opportunity to let you know our plans. But I guess you turned that around and put yourself in the center again."

His eyebrows went up. He was surprised, but he said nothing. Maybe time will heal things, I don't know. We left.

Beautiful Molly

Molly is never convinced

My lone catch

Dave and Sheri in Chicago

Lee and Will: Camping ritual

Scenic lake from our back deck

Garage party

## CHAPTER 8

# The anguish of parting

I n the Autumn of 2014, well before we saw any signs of snow, we packed up what we couldn't sell over the summer, or what we otherwise couldn't part with immediately, and placed it in a ten-by-ten storage unit. We sold the house and the furniture with it and gave away what remained. Sheri's brother Lee, coincidentally, was moving from Chicago to Houston, and at Will's request decided that they would relocate together.

Will had made it pretty clear over the summer, in his way, that he wasn't as high on the whole Hawaiian thing as maybe we were. He had voiced his worries about a lot of little things, and I could see the distance concerned him. I felt foolish assuming he would be happy just tagging along with us, trailing in the wake of whatever we were doing, when he so obviously had his own wants and wishes, and chief among them was to live near his brother.

The previous spring, a few weeks after my mother's funeral, we found a listing for a restaurant that was for sale on Kauai. So, with a move toward our future in mind, we booked a flight. Before we left I voiced my fears, which I cleverly disguised as concerns, as to why I thought a restaurant might be too big of a leap. How we should maybe start smaller and work our way into some experience and knowledge of what we wanted to do. I was allowing some of my anxiety from the past to re-surface, making me suddenly apprehensive. I was a little unnerved when faced with reality. I could get ahold of it, but right then, my conviction was waning. Sheri was neither distraught nor dismayed at the small cracks that had formed in the thin veil of my composure. She simply brushed it off and said she couldn't imagine why we couldn't do anything we wanted. That was good enough for me.

After landing, we went directly to the historic plantation town of Old Koloa, where the restaurant was located, to get an eyeful of what we might be getting ourselves into. We wandered without need or want of a guide and took in what we saw, just a cursory look to see if pursuit was necessary. It wasn't, but we still maintained an appointment with the owner later in the week.

The place turned out to be quite a bit less than what we were led to believe, and that's a kind understatement. I was surprised that they were doing business, not much by the look of things, but they were up and running so to speak. Somehow, we had completely missed this place during our past trips to Kauai, and for good reason. It was decades filthy, poorly represented, and in need of some serious maintenance. Maybe some love too. Although it enjoyed an attractive open-air setting, it lacked the vibrant tropical feeling that it demanded. The place was rundown, dirty, and depressing.

We shuffled quietly out the door and began walking to our rental car. Both of us were lost in our separate thoughts about what we just saw, processing the options that might yet be available. As a precursor to coming on this unscheduled trip to Kauai, we had already made up our minds that this is where we wanted home to be. With my mother now gone, Kauai is where we belonged. We looked at what seemed to be every opportunity there was for a restaurant, or a sandwich kiosk, even a taco stand, anything to pin hope and a dream too. From Poipu to Kalaheo, we ran our vacation like a business, a scouting trip for our future.

In the end, with our known opportunities falling short, we bought a food truck from a guy on Craig's List. He had brought it over from the mainland to start his son off in a business of his own, but the son fled the island wanting nothing to do with the proposed venture. It seemed familiar and I found myself wondering if he'd run from the business or the father. Maybe it was both.

It looked like it had just rolled off the assembly line. Everything inside was still wrapped in plastic and the stainless-steel walls were clean and polished. Fryers, grills, cold stations, freezers, sinks, and prep tables created quite a set-up, but even more so, it was a grounding stake for our imminent and absolute return to the island for our final time. I had no idea how much money could be made, or if this was even practical, and I'm not even sure it mattered. For better, or worse, we were moving to the one place that made us feel at home, that checked all the boxes on who and where we wanted to be and gave us a re-set to chase any future we could imagine. We were moving to Kauai. A local guy offered to store it on his property for a small fee until we returned, and it has never moved since.

When we arrived back at our usual lives in Michigan, we were tasked with delivering the news to our friends, that we would be selling our house and leaving. Not up north where the visits could still be mutual, not the east coast where flights are always cheap, but a quarter of the way around the world, to a tiny dot lost in the

Pacific. We were excited about the path we were taking, but our hearts also broke for those we were leaving behind.

At a dinner party in the home of one of our neighbors, I gathered the group to attention. Side by side, with drinks in hand, Sheri and I explained not just our desire, but our strange need, almost like a constant pull, to spend our life on Kauai, and make our living there. We told them about the opportunities we explored, about the restaurant that wasn't worth looking at, and finally about the food truck and our plan, thin as it was, going forward.

In the silence that followed, a combination of disbelief and shock swept across the faces of the people in front of us. If I thought too long about what we were saying, I think I would have joined them. It seemed to border on insanity. And from what I could gather from all the words leaving my mouth, we had just put common sense in the rearview mirror. Was this crazy?

Eventually, surprise flowed into heartfelt embraces, loud conversation, and a lot more tequila. Oh, and Harley proclaiming with his drink held high, that this summer would be the greatest lake party yet. His statement, given with so much juvenile lust and excitement had me wondering if we would make some sort of childhood pact before I too fell out laughing with the rest of them.

I joined in the spirit of forecasting good times by telling everyone that we had a hundred bottles of wine in our cellar and that by the end of summer, we would drink them all together. And we did. What great people we had surrounded ourselves with over the last few years. I thought this would be the hardest part of leaving, but Sheri knew for her, it wouldn't be.

On the fourth of October, 2014, we said goodbye to almost everyone we knew at a party in our empty garage. The summer had indeed been epic, every gathering seemed to find its way to the lake no matter the hour, or the company, and we laughed and cried with every friend we had. We finished the last three bottles of wine that night in a final toast to whatever lies ahead, and those memories will stay with us forever.

Some of our friends, we could tell, secretly believed that we'd be back in a year. After having reached for something else, only to find certain failure, we would return safely back to the box their mind had comfortably put us in. But I knew that if we didn't at least pursue the life that our hearts demanded, then we had already failed, and let ourselves down. Besides, I also knew, and Sheri agreed, that no matter what happened on Kauai, we would not be returning to live in Michigan. The winters are a good excuse to stay away, but there are other things also that will keep me elsewhere.

Molly, that sweet, beautiful, loving black lab with the clever personality, was on our minds the entire summer. That goofy dog had let me know early on that she would tolerate my presence as long as I was active with the tennis ball, even though she rolled her eyes at me every time I looked at her. One of her favorite games was showing you how fast she was, which also included the tennis ball and sometimes the car, and never seemed to get old. Well, for her anyway. She didn't like to wrestle, I learned that early, but she loved a good belly scratch, and make no mistake, in the end, Sheri was her best friend. But I loved her all the same.

From the time we decided to move, Sheri had been in emotional turmoil about Molly. She wanted what was best for her Molly-Moo and it broke her heart because what was best for Molly was the lake, not the ocean. It was running in her own wide-open space, chasing ducks, deer, and tennis balls, not cooped up inside and then tied to a leash. The condo life was no place for her, surrounded as it was by lava cliffs, battering waves, and a strong current. Molly would no doubt look at it as the perfect place to showcase the type of water-jumping skills she had mastered while leaping off the dock behind our house. There were too many unknowns in the life we were running to, with a schedule impossible to make, let alone keep, and a direction although aimed, fraught with uncertainty.

Molly loved cheese by the slice, snow, bacon strips and boat rides, and defending her driveway, but most of all she loved Sheri, and Sheri loved her back. She and Molly were inseparable before I came along and through our years together it remained that way. This was no short vacation, where we could pop her into the doggie daycare and know she was well attended to and cared for. This was a major change in life, and deciding what was best for Molly was part of it.

For Sheri, the thought of separation was hard enough, but pulling Molly away from the only thing she's ever known felt wrong. And finding a more than suitable home that met all of the criteria that Molly was worthy of, was at times more than she wanted to bear. In that final summer, I would often find her on the floor curled up with her dog, wet blue eyes buried in the fur of her neck, quietly stroking the soft spot of her belly and telling her what a pretty girl she was. It pained me to know that Sheri was hurting, that I could do nothing to take away the ache, except insist that Molly go with us, but that wasn't right either, and she felt that way too.

There were only a few options on the table, and while all were acceptable, none were ideal. The long flight meant that Molly would be locked in a kennel for eight hours in the belly of an airplane, and she despised being caged. She responded to it with extreme claustrophobia and exhibited a Houdini-like ability to escape, or go mad trying. So, that idea was moved to the back burner.

Sheri had sadly turned away from the idea, putting herself in Molly's paws. Coupled with the extreme change in dog lifestyle and dog surroundings, I would imagine that Molly would feel like she was convicted of a crime she didn't commit. Sentenced to life in a world where loose dogs chasing things is highly frowned upon, if not outright forbidden. She would adjust, but she would never be the same. A key element of her personality, the very running wild spirit that makes Molly want to chase anything that moves, just to go faster, would be taken from her.

Near the beginning of summer, while we were outside doing some clean-up, the neighbor's dog Malcolm, wandered into the yard and started running with Molly, sort of playing tag. Initially, we were too surprised to see another dog in our yard to try and call them apart, then we watched in equal amazement as a friendship began. Molly has never really been around other dogs, and the way she would bark off anything passing the driveway, we assumed she wouldn't be interested in a social call, but dogs have their way, I guess.

By the time Doug and Debbie drove up in their four-wheeler asking if we'd seen Malcolm, we were able to point out the two of them, exhausted and huddled in the middle of the yard together. They were as surprised as we were, and couldn't stop apologizing for his escape. We insisted that it was no problem and besides, they seem to like each other. Molly was indeed mothering poor old Malcolm. In the time we've known them, our two dogs had never been together. Our properties being separated as they were, both dogs seemed content to abide in their own space.

We met Doug and Deb about a year earlier when they moved into the house next to us. Their property was a good two acres of marshland further along the lakeshore, so it was kind of a stretch to say they were next door, I mean, we weren't shaking hands across the fence. Nevertheless, true to the people that they are, they caught us in the driveway one day and suggested that we come over for cocktails. The night turned into four bottles of wine and three fingers of Jameson, lasting until an embarrassing three a.m. I couldn't believe it when Sheri told me the time, I thought it was no later than midnight. The conversation had made us instant friends and that night the clock had no meaning. I think we'll miss them the most, maybe because we knew them the least, in terms of time anyway.

In the following months, the two dogs spent more and more time together. I think it was Deb's plan all along to show Sheri that Molly was good for Malcolm, that she could and would be comfortable with them. And happy. Because Debbie knew that was exactly what Sheri needed more than anything else. She knew the struggle and the turmoil she was going through, possibly because Malcolm was growing old and not well. It was more likely that as a nurse, she knew that to begin to comfort someone, you had to make them comfortable with who and what was around them, and help put their mind at ease.

So, after gently allowing Sheri to see that Molly could adjust to a new life and still be Molly, they asked us if we would allow them the pleasure of giving Molly a new home. Sheri, who had voiced this same thought to me a few days before, wrapped her arms around Doug and softly cried against his shoulder.

"If something changes you can have her back anytime you want. Just know that we're going to love her and take care of her exactly as you would. And I'm so happy to see what Molly has done for Malcolm." Debbie said.

"Thank you, both of you, this has been so…" She didn't have the words.

"Emotional, Heart wrenching, stressful." Doug stepped in. "Deb and I saw it, we know. This is what we want for you guys, for us, for Malcolm. Hell, I'm excited, Molly's a great dog. When you guys finally decide to leave, we'll bring her down here and you won't have anything to worry about. Well, with Molly anyway."

It was oddly enough their son Josh, living in Chicago, who finally decided on the day that we would leave. After the party Saturday, we had planned to depart the next afternoon to begin the cross-country journey to Oakland. Lee had sold his house in Chicago, but he and Will were still there for another week before they headed down to Houston for Lee's job transfer. Sheri and I were staying the first night with them at his house, and having dinner in the city as a farewell to what was. At least with them, time and distance will never bring erosion and decay.

We had two tickets to paradise leaving from Oakland, California. Our Jeep was scheduled at the port the day before our flight to begin its journey across the Pacific, where if all went well out there on those rough and anxious waters, we would be reunited in Kauai. All of this was taking place at the end of October, so we had a couple of weeks of open road and big skies to look forward to. Eventually, we planned to end up on the western edge of Oregon where we could drive the coast all the way to San Francisco, camping along the way. We just couldn't seem to find the courage to take that first step, it was so freaking scary to just drive away. But that was all that was left.

On Sunday, I woke up with a slight hangover and wasn't sure I was ready to just jump right into action. I settled on an easy pace, loading what I could into the Jeep. I took some notes on last-minute things we needed on the way out, double-checked a few things around the house that now belonged to someone else, and tried to look busy. Sheri was showing no inclination towards giving Molly up just yet, and I didn't push the issue. Before I knew it, it was too late to leave for Chicago and expect to arrive at a reasonable hour, so Sheri called Lee and told him we would be there the following night.

Monday was more of the same. I swept the garage for some reason, we did some shopping for the trip, and our neighbors were continually surprised that we hadn't left yet. Honestly, we were too. Sheri decided the carpet on the stairs needed shampooing. It's funny what our minds will focus on when we're trying to avoid something else. And this is something we had planned and worked for. It was something we wanted. We were finding that leaving everything we've ever known behind and testing who we are, and what we're capable of doing, was proving to be daunting.

When I came in from the garage and saw what she was involved with, we both started laughing. She was standing on towels drying some of the stair treads. We laughed because we knew what this was, holding on for one last moment to what is known, what has been a part of our lives for so long, the comfortable. The doorway to a future that we were creating held no clear signage or informa-tion about what lay beyond, and it beckoned. But it also caused us to stutter and freeze at the threshold. Just then Sheri's phone rang. The contact said it was Josh, so she put it on speaker.

"Hey Josh, your back." He was away on a thing for work and missed the party.

"I was just talking to my mom and she said you haven't brought Molly down there yet. I thought you guys were leaving on Sunday." No preamble, just straight to the point.

"Oh, yeah…"

"Things to do…"

"We were just now packing…" We talked over each other, battling for excuses. I think I mentioned that Sheri had to shampoo the carpets.

"Sorry I couldn't come up last weekend, but this might work out even better." He said.

"Okay? What do you mean?"

"Well, tomorrow night is the only night I have free for a week, so if you take some time with Molly down at mom and dads in the morning and then head to Chicago, we can meet for dinner at Greek Islands. Bring Lee and Will, we'll celebrate." He left no room for debate.

"Okay, I guess we can do that, we were starting to drift, this helps. Thanks, Josh, we would love to see you." Our enthusiasm was genuine.

"Perfect, I'll meet you out front at seven, corner of Halsted and Adam's. I'll text you the address, can't wait to see you."

And then he was gone. We continued to stare at the phone like he might change his mind, before realizing he had hung up. He never gave us a chance to lightly protest, or offer an appeal concerning the proper day to finally leave. It was the push out the door that we needed to finally let go. We shipped nothing to the island, and we loaded into the back of the Jeep, only four large duffle bags. Two contained nothing but camping gear, and two held some clothes and a few belongings that were coming with us, my grandfather's Purple Heart among them. We were truly starting over.

We walked Molly down the street and said goodbye to Deb again as she was the only one home. We also thanked her for what we believed was her part in Josh's phone call. She feigned ignorance, and that was okay. After a difficult parting with 'the world's most beautiful dog', we left for Chicago.

Two days after we all met for dinner in Chicago we were in Lee's driveway, hugging and saying goodbye again, with the promise that he and Will would come to Kauai soon. It was hard to separate, knowing it would likely be a long time before we saw them again, but we would. Had we remained where we were, while Lee made his move to Houston, we would have been happy to drive down there and make an annual vacation out of it. Now the ocean seemed an impenetrable barrier.

We planned to wander across the top of the country and take in the northern states. We drove thru endless prairies, watercolor landscapes, and ceaseless miles of nothing but harvested fields. I found a road that looped through several miles of the alien barrens, known as the Badlands, a terrain so desolate and puzzling that it removed my sense of where I was. It was like a moonscape in a nightmare.

From there we slipped through the Black Hills, past the soaring Tetons, and over the Rockies through Beartooth pass. We spent a few days in Yellowstone and watched as Old Faithful lived up to its namesake, before finally reaching the towering Redwood forests of California. Our aimless drive took us through towns with names like Custer and Crazy Horse, Big Horn, and Lodge Grass. As well as detours to Wind Cave, Devil's Tower, and of course, those four Presidents chiseled into the side of a mountain. Two weeks after the beginning of a long and memorable drive across the country, we were settling into our seats for a one-way flight to Kauai.

It was the absolute unknown that made this last trip so exciting, and so terrifying at the same moment. I was a ball of nerves. We both were. My insides were churning like a blender set to low speed. From that moment on, we knew that life was going to be a totally different experience. For the first time, life was going to be what we made it, and it would change in ways we couldn't imagine. As it turned out, we had no idea what we were in for.

## CHAPTER 9

# Not the welcome we anticipated

The plane finally banked for its final approach into Lihue, the county seat for the small island of Kauai. The beautiful Kipu Mountain range became visible out my cabin window; Ha'upu, with its usual toupee of clouds, marking its path to the harbor. My heart stirred. I couldn't believe we were there, that we were really doing this. All my emotions were shouting to have their say, each clamoring to be heard above the near frenzied pitch of the others. While excitement and awe held their own in the beginning, fear and panic seemed to be winning the day.

We left the airport in a smothering wet blanket of tropical humidity. Hurricane Ana was winding down in the Pacific, west of the islands, and sucking up any breeze that might remotely affect us. The air was suffocating and we were tired from the early morning flight. Since the Jeep wouldn't arrive for three weeks, we picked up a rental car and headed to the south side of the island.

Sheri was busy answering a few tedious e-mails that related to her job, while I tried to decipher the controls on the air conditioner. With the stifling heat, we wouldn't last long with the windows down. She was planning to continue servicing her customers for another year to help us get started, before handing them off to another agent at her company. It was mostly e-mails and paperwork, but the distance was proving to be a challenge on day one.

Our destination was a condo on the south shore about five minutes from the small plantation town of Koloa. It's the same place we refused to stay at while on vacation, and the same one, that upon arriving on Kauai, we now had control of. It had sat empty since the final vacationers left earlier in the month. I had never seen the place, but I knew from pictures that it would need some work, not a lot, but enough.

When we arrived, we found the reception to be as oppressive as the weather. The windows and sliding doors had been left open by the woman who did the cleaning for God knows how long, probably two weeks by the look of things. Everything was covered in a grimy layer of moist salt air and red dirt. The stone tiles on the floor were slippery and repulsive. Our little home, left unattended, was becoming a damp cave.

I can tell you that religion, or spirituality, isn't a trait of mine, or my wife's for that matter, but I do believe in a bigger something. I believe in fate, but I also believe that some elements and steps ultimately lead us to fate. I believe in karma, good and bad, and what comes around goes around. I believe that sometimes we're led by a mysterious force that can't be explained, one that demands all of your attention and seems to guide your decisions, something that drives you and you don't know why. Like Sheri and I were inexplicably compelled to make a life on Kauai.

As we both stood there in shock, taking in the dirty walls and dull film that covered everything, we passed a knowing look between us. I could see that we were simultaneously replaying the day, from the jet lag to the heat, to the sudden problems that had come up through Sheri's office, and now this. I think the idea hit us both at the same time that this was a test, albeit in the scope of life a small one, but still a test.

My mind flashed back to Johnny, a local guy we met and began a friendship with the last time we were here on Kauai. He told us the island decides who stays and who doesn't. That it tests and tries everyone who comes to live there, shaking the very foundation of their life and throwing them off balance. He spoke it in his heavy island pidgin, but I was able to grasp the idea. I always thought that it was just the natural course of life and the decisions that alter it that did that, but I kind of liked his cool island theory. Over the course of the next few months, however, I not only bought into what he was saying, I became a majority stockholder.

Within the first week, while still putting our house in order, we had driven east, to Kapa'a, to survey the location of where the un-named food truck would do business. Seven months before, we had put down a small deposit to hold this spot until we arrived in October. They said that, within that time, it was going to be a nice courtyard between the main road and the bike path. Other vendors, they said, would make up two curved rows opposite each other, open on the ends like a carnival midway. We were thinking the theme would be something cute and islandy, a place with a good vibe that would immediately catch the eye.

As we turned off the main road and crunched to a halt, we found a gravel parking lot with three other food trucks littering the ground. Only one appeared to be open, and its operator was sleeping in a chair out front. I could see that the vision that had been put forth to us had not even begun to be realized. The place was a nightmare. From the moment I stepped out of the car, I wanted to leave. I couldn't put a finger on it in a logical sense, but there was something wrong with the ground I was standing on.

When you visit Kauai and travel up the west side of the island, or drive the road that takes you along the Wailua River, you will feel an energy that is hard to describe. It's nothing mystical, just a slight tingling of the skin and a heightened sense of calm, of awareness, a feeling that something important happened here, and it demands that you stand in awe. Kauai is special, there are other places on the island that are like that, giving off good mana. This dusty parking lot, however, was not one of them.

The woman we were there to meet, a leasing agent representing the property, stepped away from her battered Toyota pickup and came over to introduce herself. With the formalities out of the way she wasted no time explaining that if we wanted to keep the spot, we would need to sign a rental agreement and begin paying the lease in November.

She mentioned nothing about the proposed improvements, and instead, brought us up to date on things that were our responsibility. Amid her clatter of information, we learned that the developer had backed out, and only three power and water connections had been run to the weed-strewn lot, and they were already in use. To install the necessary utilities, we were required to contract the county to do the work, and file the necessary permits, all at our expense. She carried on about location and sight lines, Kapa'a shopping, accessibility to the bike path, and on and on. I was tuning out quickly, and I could see by a glance, that Sheri was too.

Aside from the fact that the whole place had a decidedly creepy feel to it, I couldn't believe they expected us to pay for their infrastructure. We had never seen the location, as we were corresponding by e-mail, but they had clearly outlined all their plans for the food court. If you're coming over in October they said, all of that would be ready. But it wasn't, not even close, and the fact was, that it never would be.

Digging deeper there was the problem of parking, it was minimal and that was being generous. All those cars traveling past on the main road might look like a built-in cash stream, but they wouldn't have a place to park even if they did stop. And since it was already the lunch hour, from what I was seeing, it didn't look like they would. It's so far north of the shopping district that people don't often walk up that way, and the bike path didn't seem to be a very sustainable way to stay in business either.

We both knew, just by looking around and getting a feel for the place, that this was not the answer to our life on Kauai. Something more than just desire had drawn us to this island and we were, at that moment, utterly unsure of what that something was. But one thing we knew without question, this location wasn't it.

The deposit we had given to the management company was happily left behind just for the sake of getting off that eerie and unkempt piece of land. We parted pleasantly with the woman we had met there, having apparently obtained all the information we would need. We hugged, as is custom, and she said that if she didn't hear from us by the end of the month, she was giving the spot to someone else, which couldn't possibly be true. We thanked her, and I hauled ass out of there.

I told Sheri, as we were briskly turning onto Prince Kuhio, that if we set up our food truck there, in that spot, we would fail. Yes, I was terrified of taking that next step, but that place felt wrong, I couldn't tell you how or why, beyond the obvious, but it did. Nothing of what I saw brought a vision of success. It had all the atmosphere of a prison sentence, with a low wall bordering the bike path and covered in graffiti as the backdrop.

As we drove back to the south side of the island, we spent much of that time in silence, both of us organizing and cataloging what was on our minds. When we finally did speak, it was at the same time and all at once. In the end, we agreed that the current location for the food truck was not a viable option. With Sheri still working remotely for a year, even with all its headaches, we had time to explore other more feasible locations or see what different possibilities might present themselves.

As we slipped through the final months of that year and into the next, we kept ourselves busy with the condo, made a few contacts, and met some good people on the island. We were settling into our life on Kauai and trying to figure out what that life was going to be.

From the beginning, we faced challenges that we hadn't even known were there. The generally dim perception of outsiders by the locals, the nearly impenetrable doorway to a lease that kept us from finding a business location, and the skepticism of almost everyone we had so far shared our ideas with, were just a few. There were so many annoying little obstacles that forced us to alter not only much of our way of life but also much of our way of thinking. We were testing the island as much as it was testing us, pushing and probing as to where we would plant our roots. We were determined to make our life here and in doing so, to make some type of positive impact on the community around us.

We discovered over and over again while trying to find a suitable location for our nameless food truck, that the county was simply not issuing enough permits to landowners who were eager to accommodate a growing industry. After running into one dead end after another, Sheri reworked and re-wrote our business plan for the food truck, and expanded it to reflect a moderate-sized restaurant. We began to look in other directions.

We contacted a couple of restaurants looking to sell and met with the owners, but nothing fit. We talked to a few malls in the area with lease space available, but the fact that we had never owned or operated a restaurant was an understandable source of concern, and we were turned away.

It got a little frustrating, on an island that seemed full of opportunities, that we had yet to make the right connection. With our minds bent on how we could make the food truck work, we weren't allowing ourselves to look beyond those boundaries at what could be a much bigger picture. But we kept going back to the idea and meeting the same problems, jamming the square peg in the round hole.

As the new year kicked off with a surprisingly stunning fireworks show at Poipu Beach, Sheri and I were talking about expanding our view. We decided that if that's what it took to allow us to make our home on Kauai, then we were willing to sacrifice our vision for a time and take on the challenge of running any type of small business. If given the right opportunity, we could, at least, build from there.

Later that week we had an appointment to sit down with yet another management company. This one handled property on the East and South ends of the island, including the town of Koloa, five minutes from where we lived. By this point, we were ready with a plan for just about any possibility, and more than ready to begin working. With our notes and numbers in hand, we were poised to meet what might await us.

We had found a pattern of peace and clear thought while sitting quietly by the ocean and brainstorming ideas for the future. We talked through and created a plan for everything from restaurants to retail. Those moments we spent losing ourselves in the brilliance of the endless blue Pacific eased our minds and raised our hopes, which we needed because that and a handful of papers were all we were taking into this meeting.

We met Allan around a large conference table that seemed to be the size of a football field. It took up too much space for any single room, so it sat in the foyer of an unused rear entrance. It could have easily held three separate meetings, in confidence. So, with virtually no experience in anything we were asking them to write us a lease for, we couldn't have felt any smaller than we did at that table.

Allan was shuffling papers around and stood to greet us with a handshake. He wasn't a tall man, but he carried himself a foot above his normal height, not arrogance, but assurance, a certainty in himself. He looked to be in his upper-seventies, with a veil of perfectly combed white hair parted on the side. He directed us to sit down and quickly retrieved a silver tray holding a pitcher of water, and some plastic cups from a side table.

After introductions and a little small talk, in which we learned of Allan's love for surfing and how, incredibly, he still surfs the old man's break at Waiohai, he got down to why we were there. He had set aside the stack of papers that were in front of him because he could see that we were well armed with our own bundle.

"What do you think I can do for you?" He began.

"Well, I guess that's what we're here to find out. Hopefully something, maybe everything." I said.

He laughed with good humor, hearing that before, no doubt.

"Was there a particular location you had in mind? How much space do you need?"

"What I'd like to do," Sheri said, "is take you through our business plan for a restaurant, and share our ideas with you, what we'd like to see happen, and how we can work together. Then you can tell us what you have, if anything."

"Okay, we can do that. Were you thinking of something in Lihue, on this side?" He asked.

"No, more like Koloa." I piped in.

"Hmm, I don't believe we have anything available in Koloa, at least not for a restaurant. Although… well, never mind. I could show you something in Lihue this week." He said apologetically.

Speaking too soon perhaps, a shadow crossed his face and he seemed to think of something. For a split second, he looked to be measuring what he would say next, possibly in fear of stirring our hope. Maybe he wasn't at liberty to reveal anything about the pause in his statement that he could see so piqued our interest. With the debate settled in his mind, he focused his attention.

"If you can wait, maybe in a month or two, there might be something in Koloa that we could look at, but that's up in the air. In the meantime, we've got a lot of ground to cover. We'll need to look at all your financials and what you're bringing as collateral. We need to look at what your plan is, and what you intend to sell, or do, from the location. All of that comes first before we can make a decision on whether or not to present you with a lease, of course. Did you say you had a restaurant now?"

"Not at the moment, no." Sheri deflected.

Before he could respond, she quickly continued by laying out pages in front of him. It was the business plan, figures, notes, and ideas we had put together for our tropical restaurant.

"I want to go through this with you, and if there's anything that doesn't make sense, point it out so I can explain it better, or we can figure out how to fix it. Maybe it will help narrow down what kind of a space we need"

"Rite on." Was all he said.

For the next hour, Sheri and I weaved an intricate web of numbers, philosophy, passion, and our drive to succeed. Allan was answering his own questions by looking at the sheets that were collecting in front of him. At a break in the conversation, while he was skimming one of the pages, he asked us if there was anything that would draw us back to the mainland, back to Michigan, as if we might just pick up and leave suddenly in the middle of a lease.

The answer, of course, was no. But everyone says no. So, I told him that my mother had passed away, and that was my last tether. I have a sister I've seen twice in twenty years, and my father has become strange, going his own way. Sheri had only her brothers, scattered around the country, living their own lives. He looked satisfied.

We led him through a preliminary menu, including everything that could be acquired from the island, and overwhelmed him with our thoughts on décor. We talked about live music, and how to present it. We kept rolling from one topic to the next, our hearts dripping off our sleeves. Finally, having discovered my background, Allan asked the simplest, most obvious question of the day; why don't you open a plumbing shop? It seems like everyone needs a plumber. I told him simply that I had done it long enough, it was time for a new challenge and a new life. I told him this is not only where we belonged, it's where we were meant to do something else. He seemed to understand.

He was able to glean through various parts of our conversation that I had a few skills beyond plumbing. That when it came to carpentry, I could build, or re-build just about anything. Back in Michigan, I turned our tired, old kitchen into something out of a magazine. When he asked me about cooking, I told him I was quite at home in front of a flame, with a pair of tongs. He took it in with a thoughtful mind as if some of those skills might be useful later.

We warmed to each other, the three of us, like family, like we wanted this man to be proud of us, and for him to know that there was value here. That's the impact he made on us. And I had hoped, in turn, that we had somehow impacted him as well. With our options all but dwindling to nothing, it was looking like Allan was our final hope to secure a lease before we fully invested in the food truck.

By the time the meeting was over, we had said everything we wanted to say, and I think we had earned Allan's respect. I know he earned ours. A lot of people we had met since moving to the island, and really quite a few back home, were insistent that we would never acquire a lease, especially for a restaurant, without at least some prior background in the business. It will never happen seemed to be the final word. We were finding truth in that, as it turned out to be a sticking point with other management companies, even as we delivered the same scorching passion.

Allan walked us to the door, stowing the copies of everything we had given him into a green folder, which he tucked securely under his left arm. He said it was the most interesting meeting he's had in a long time, and he was so glad that he had met us. He went on to say that he was impressed with what was presented and that he would go over the facts and figures with his partner over the coming days.

Allan said he'd get back to us in a couple of weeks when he had a clearer picture of something that was developing. What that was, he wouldn't say, but he did say we might be perfect for it. He gave us a command to send them any financial paperwork they asked for, and in a timely manner. Eventually, he would get back to us with their decision one way or the other.

We left with a final handshake and a feeling of elation, a lightness we didn't have going in there. If you looked at what we were tangibly leaving with, the meeting produced very little. But in the bigger picture, it allowed us to connect to a man who had known us only a couple of hours and pull him into our empty corner. Although we drove away without even the hint of a lease offer, we still felt like we had made a breakthrough, that finally, someone was standing up with us.

We still had no idea where we were going, what future we might build, or what our minds were soon to be occupied with, but at least now there was a door ajar, with light shining through the crack, that we could just get our foot in. After nearly three months of sparing with the island for the right to live there, each time getting back up when another brick wall hit us, or maintaining our determination when defeat looked imminent, we finally had a potential opportunity within our grasp.

With essentially nowhere else to turn, we waited. Not quietly though. We spoke to Allan on the phone just to stay in touch. We e-mailed, we sent statements, account information, figures, and ideas, maybe too much. But we wanted him to know that we were extremely motivated, and a gamble on his side was also a gamble on ours.

After a month of waiting, which seemed to stretch far beyond that, we met Allan at his request at a Starbucks in Poipu. With our coffee secured we made our way out of the crowded café and found a table in the courtyard. Once we were seated, he pulled from his briefcase a stack of papers, joined together with large binder clips, and laid it on the table in front of us. I was stunned. What was sitting there, fluttering in the light breeze, could only be the archaic phrasing of the million words contained in a commercial lease. Our hearts were racing, but our minds were slow to catch up.

"This is just a sample lease you understand, we can go over this as an outline of what you can expect, and work out the details later before we write the final copy." He explained in his easy manner.

"Wait a minute, hold on a second, are you saying you're offering us a lease? On what? Where? I thought you were here to tell us that you didn't have anything, that we somehow didn't qualify. I'm…" Sheri finished, running out of words.

"Oh! I'm sorry, I thought Keith had e-mailed you. When I sent you a text about getting together, I assumed you knew we were going over the lease. Your business plan was good, and all your numbers are in order, seems to work for everyone, and we like your ideas. We're ready to work with you, and we have restaurant space opening up in Koloa. I think you guys would be the right fit."

"I can't believe this," I said. "I have no idea what to say, thank you. You won't regret this. Thank you."

"You can begin on March first. We'll meet over there together and have a proper look at the place. Until you sign the final lease you can still back out. And by the way, don't thank me too quickly, the space, as you'll see, needs a lot of tenant improvements. You're going to be quite busy." He said with a smile.

"Who cares? You're offering us a place in Koloa, we love that little town," I said.

"Then I'm sure you're familiar with the old Tomcats."

Sheri and I immediately turned to each other in surprise and a quick bark of laughter escaped as if sharing an inside joke. We conveyed to each other in that moment what we would voice later, that somehow, without our intervention, fate played its hand. The island winds, through our perseverance, had blown favorably in our direction.

As it turned out, it was the same location we had flown to Kauai to look at a year ago. We could have poured our savings into the purchase of this same failing restaurant, with nothing left over to fix what was desperately needed, let alone create the vision we wanted. The town is special, the location of the restaurant was excellent, but for what was being offered, the cost had been too high and we walked away. We knew then, that as badly as we wanted to be in Kauai, that was not the opportunity. Now, it seemed we could have it for no more than a signature on a piece of paper. We could put our money where it belonged.

"Whoa! We looked at that, the guy had it for sale last year so we came over to see it, but after a look around we told him no. How did you fix the floor, by the way?" Sheri said.

The whole point of that trip to Kauai the year before, was to look at a restaurant that on paper, seemed too good to be true, and in person, couldn't possibly live up to the asking price, so we had walked out under a cloud of discouragement. However, while meeting with the owner and his wife at a quiet table, a bit of excitement took place. I had just broken the news that there was no way we were buying his restaurant no matter how many ways he moved the numbers around when chaos erupted in the kitchen.

Our meeting had reached its end. With my declaration made, I slid their folder of unverified profit and loss statements across the table and stood to leave. A few days earlier we had covertly staked out the place and had already made up our minds. The meeting was merely a courtesy. If we had second thoughts, which we didn't, the rumbling at our feet and the Filipino cook sprinting to our table would have settled it. In a heated rush, he ran over to where we were sitting, waving his arms and speaking very fast, using broken English mixed with pantomime to express his concern. He was saying that the kitchen fell.

Looking around confused, we all went to the scene, and sure enough, a beam underneath the floor had broken. It caused one end of the small kitchen to drop about six inches, and shoved all the equipment together up against that wall, pulling the gas lines with it. I had definitely seen enough and we ran for the door. I could see by the way the place was kept, that if it hadn't been somewhat dangerous, they probably would have left the equipment like that.

I was interested to see how the repair was made, so I stopped by the following morning to see if I could be of any help, maybe cap a water or drain line for them. I assumed it would be a few days to rebuild the floor and tile it. Once inside, I found a few members of the crew moving in dirty equipment and re-attaching gas lines that should have been replaced years ago.

It took a second for my brain to process what my eyes were seeing, as it was unexpected. When the two finally connected, I was left shaking my head. They had removed all the equipment the night before, and from what I could see, had then shoveled in about four-hundred pounds of concrete to fill the gap and level the floor. They were re-assembling the kitchen on rough cement that had never seen a trowel, only slapped in place with the back of a shovel.

It was one of the craziest things I've ever seen. Nobody in their right mind could think this was a good idea, adding even more weight to an already compromised floor structure. But there it was. We found out through the process of taking over the space that the business was largely in debt, and most of that to the landlord, so it didn't take much deduction to add up all the reasons why they were no longer in business. Now, as we sat with Allan in the morning sunshine, it appeared that in just a few short weeks, I was going to see it again. Was the shoveled-in cement a temporary fix? Would there now be a solid, level floor, finished with a non-slip commercial tile? I guess I'd have to wait to find out.

"What floor?" Asked Allen. "Nobody said anything about any floor problems over there."

Or maybe I just received my answer. It didn't matter, no discussion on our part was necessary, we were determined to make anything work, even if it first required some repair. Sitting in that courtyard, however, we couldn't have possibly imagined the amount of work that was ahead of us.

## CHAPTER 10

# The money pit

On the first day of March 2015, we met Allan at the location formerly known as Tomcats in Old Koloa Town. We entered the restaurant through the cluttered front doors to the rotting smell of old fryer grease and possibly a broken sewer pipe somewhere. Between the condition of the surroundings, and the evidence of a quick move out, it looked as if a flighty, and capricious hurricane had blown through and only affected this particular structure. It hadn't changed much from the year before when we saw it last.

We were walking around making a list of notes that were already exceeding three pages, and discussing who would pay for what, when I suddenly fell through the floor in front of the walk-in cooler. Although it was odd that it would pick that moment to suddenly tilt and send me dancing for balance, after continuing the tour it didn't surprise me. Tip-toeing around behind the bar, the server's area, and the prep and dish room, we encountered enough spongy floor to make me wonder how anyone mapped their way around. There were so many pitfalls. Looking at the floor, what we thought would be a simple sub-floor replacement and new tile, now that the place was closed, turned into the largest project on our list.

With our lease in place and our plans and designs for what we had in mind submitted, we set to the task of building our future. The project, while daunting, seemed pretty straightforward, so we figured we could handle all the work ourselves. Because of the licenses I held in Michigan, the County agreed that as long as all the necessary permits were pulled and inspections done, which they were, we could move forward.

The chore proved overwhelming on the first day and with so many pages filled with so much to do, we found ourselves unable to focus on one thing at a time. I would haul debris that was gathering in one area to the dumpster only to find myself on the next trip back in suddenly ripping into a wall that was shrouded in mold. Or pulling up a piece of floor that was rotted beyond dangerous. I was going in circles, trying to do everything at once and essentially accomplishing nothing. I could see, like with everything else in life, that we needed to organize this thing and create a plan of attack.

Sheri, unable to resist following the same format, was working hard and accomplishing as little as I was. She had turned her focus to other parts of the restaurant and was busy peeling off old stickers, cleaning the walls, and pulling nails that once held up the frames and collages of someone else's memories, someone else's past. Tearing off beaten and battered trim boards suddenly popped up on her list. She'd switch tactics now and again and I'd find her swinging a broom at sticky clouds of cobwebs that were lurking in every corner, or armed with a sanding block going after one of the ancient stains that decorated the wood floors in the dining rooms. She was wearing out the same circular pattern that I was.

Later, when the sun was sinking low, and promising another brilliant and colorful sunset over sparkling waters, we took a walk to our favorite spot by the ocean. This had become an almost nightly ritual dating back to the day that we quite literally stumbled upon it. We were picking our way through the rocks one afternoon, trying to get as close to the water as we could when I stumbled, executed some sort of pirouette, and landed in the very spot I was now heading for. All without spilling a single drop of bourbon. It's not a sandy and glamorous beach, nor a swinging hammock stretched between two palms, but rather a cliffside formed by tumbled and fallen pieces of lava to create a rocky coastline. In that jumble of ancient stones, we discovered a natural seating area, with a place to put our feet up and proper end tables to set a drink on. It was a design so natural and so in tune with its surroundings that no sculptor, with mallet and chisel in hand, could have ever created it.

In our little hideaway, down below the bluff and even further below the condo we lived in, signs of civilization diminished, and the limitless Pacific Ocean commanded our view and attention. Among the swimming and diving sea turtles, the jumping and spinning dolphins, and if the season was right, the mighty Humpbacks splashing their tails and teaching their young to do whale things, we would plan and discuss our future.

This had become our place to hide, think, devise, and dream. To create a narrative for what remained of our lives, with the ubiquitous crashing waves as a continuous soundtrack. In our conversations throughout the day, it was already decided that we needed two things immediately. First and foremost was an extra pair of hands. We needed someone who could use a hammer and a power saw without me teaching them. Someone who had a chunk of free time that they wouldn't mind getting paid for.

I cast my mind around the town of Koloa and our neighborhood, thinking of possible suspects, none fit the complete profile, though there were a few questionable guys that came close. I figured we'd go over it once we had a drink and a nice view in front of us. However, while crossing the parking lot on the way to our secret spot, we bumped into Johnny.

We had met John the year before, on our final vacation to Kauai. I'll never forget his passion for music, hunched over a guitar while sitting on a bench playing island songs for us. We were re-acquainted a few days after we arrived on the island, in the open stairway that leads to our unit. He was painting the handrail a rich brown. We remembered him, of course. A personality that strong doesn't hide in the shadows. He immediately recognized us as well and we met with a hug. He seemed surprised that we had actually moved there, and said so.

The year before, in a pavilion at Poipu beach, he told us to call him Johnnylove. Just like that, all one word. We were drawn to his charisma and open friendship. He told us that he was born on the island and his family could be traced back several generations. He claimed many times that he was half Hawaiian, or *hapa*, on his mother's side. Only in his smooth island tongue, it came out sounding more like, "I get plenty Hawaiian you know. On my mudda side."

It was the first time Sheri, or I had ever held a conversation with someone whose speech was heavily weighted with the Hawaiian pidgin that is so predominant in Kauai. His way of talking came to me in bits and pieces at times, like I was listening to a rap song. All the elements of the English language were there, just mixed up, as if everything he said was poured out of a box and fell randomly into sentences. His voice had a melody and a cadence that was beautiful. I was fascinated.

He discovered that we were here to figure out what was next, and live our lives, and we learned that he worked for our complex in the maintenance department. Through that almost daily interaction, we became friends, the three of us, and Johnnylove slowly taught us what it meant to live there. It was not a place we were born and raised, but we love that island and the people on it enough to desire a place in the community. Johnny helped guide us through the world of the locals, and we met a lot of great people that we may not have otherwise come in contact with, and we were becoming comfortable with what was around us and really feeling at home.

It was the feeling at home part that my mind was dwelling on, as Sheri and I walked toward the small gate that would take us on a rough path to the ocean. All the work immediately ahead of us was everything I've ever known, it was ground that I had trod a thousand times, and it was comfortable. It allowed me, for a time, to safely bar the door in my mind that threatened to burst open with panic. If I lingered too long at that door, I could hear straining at the hinges and hideous whispers.

My brain constantly rattled through questions. What makes you think you can open a restaurant? How are you going to set up the kitchen, or the bar, or prep? What about menus? What about a chef? Signage? Advertising? Who is going to train the staff? What positions are needed? How does the whole process even come together?" And so many more that at times, it took all my will to hold that door shut. But I couldn't take on all those things right away, I had to work this in stages, and right now we simply needed someone to help us.

"Hoy! Kawika, how you stay, bruddah! Aloha, Sheri."

He's compelled to address me with my Hawaiian name, and never anything else.

"Johnnylove my man, how's it going? Whoa, you don't look so good." I said.

"I stay piss off aready, as why."

"Okay, I'm sorry, what happened, I mean, what's wrong?" When he's mad about something, or drunk, his brown skin gets just a hue of red, and his eyes start blinking at top speed. He didn't appear to be drinking yet, so I assumed the former.

"Eh. They no can talk to me dat way, I get plenty respec, you know, I walk out. They no respec for me. Not right."

"So, what, you quit then?"

"I no can work for deez guys, treat me like one dog. Up da stairs, down da stairs, how come you never like sweep the pool? Why you no work Sundays? I get church you know. Not right, no can speak to someone dat way. I get rights, uh. I'm no more gonna take dat shit. Not right, deez guys."

"That sucks, I'm sorry John. So, are you saying you quit?" He's had a running feud with someone in the office about something unknowable, I guess, maybe respect, or the lack thereof, and frankly, I was surprised that he had lasted through the winter. Meanwhile, I'm thinking I just found the guy I need.

"I'm over it, I walk off." He said.

"Well, do you want to start helping us rebuild the restaurant? I can pay you. And I need you."

Johnny's rants often included 'the man holding us down', which in his eyes meant foreigners, typically white foreigners, known as haoles, coming over from the mainland, taking all the jobs, and buying up all the land. To his point, the Kauai of his youth, or his father's youth, was not the Kauai of today. But then nowhere is. With that said, I figured he'd appreciate the fact that I needed him, being a haole myself.

He didn't hesitate or balk at the idea like I thought he might in the rattled state that he was already in. His countenance brightened and his whole demeanor relaxed, and with a Hawaiian handshake that was pulled into an embrace, we agreed on how much I could pay him each day, and when to show up in the morning. We parted with the standard 'Aloha', and the usual vow of 'see you tomorrow', and with that, we both walked away with just a little brighter outlook.

So, with the first of two immediate needs, surprisingly and unexpectedly met, we could focus our attention on what I thought was our second imperative. It was simple, really, when you look at all we had faced since arriving here, and all that was yet to come. We both knew that we couldn't continue the whole chaotic run, from project to project, trying to accomplish everything at once on a list that was long to start with, and had over one day, grown longer.

We found our place and began our ritual of staring at the ocean. I couldn't stop talking about the good fortune of running into Johnnylove in the parking lot. He was exactly the person we needed, with skills that went beyond anything I had hoped for. I could barely contain myself. Sheri, meanwhile, was leafing through a dog-eared notebook that she had been dragging around. After finding a blank page about three-quarters in, we begin the much-needed task of giving some order and semblance to this growing beast that had chained itself to our future. By the time we were done, the sun had set and we were somehow on our lanai, drinking mai-tai's.

In the process, we managed to break down the big list into a lot of smaller ones, detailing each project and filling several pages.

Some of the sheets held claim to the mountain of materials and supplies that would come from Home Depot and other places around the island. Most were lined with musings and wanderings, and thoughts about décor and atmosphere.

A dusty cloud was swept from my mind and by having a plan of attack on paper, I had a visual map, like a blueprint, to guide the progress of this remodel. It turned out to be nothing more than one big list framed into a bunch of smaller ones, but it worked. It helped us dig down to the basics to find focus and perspective on the project going forward. I'm a fan of the list.

It only took three days for the rebuild to take a serious turn for the worst. John and I had pretty much cleared out all the surface debris over the past couple of days, pulling down rotted half walls and dividers, and crumbling sheetrock. Sheri was busy hauling armloads of wreckage out the back to a second ten-yard dumpster that had been dropped off the night before.

As we began to tackle the floor, I made a hole big enough to access the two-foot-deep crawlspace below. After dispelling the darkness by switching on a halogen flood lamp, I gazed around in awe. I took a lot of photos and I still can't believe what I was seeing. Every single joist, designed originally to hold the floor up, was completely rotted through. Some in several places. Beams spaced six feet apart were crumbling and termite riddled. The one running under the kitchen was toppled where the floor had fallen in the previous year, and nothing was done to support it. I had no idea how this whole affair managed to stay up. Scrambling on my hands and knees I got out of there quickly.

I emerged from my explorations, having earlier laid down enough cardboard to cover the disgusting dirt on which I had to crawl, with my head shaking. I couldn't believe how neglected the place was and it seemed the more we dug, the worse it got. John and Sheri had continued to haul debris out to the dumpster while I was under there, so they failed to hear my R-rated exclamations and shouts of amazement. They looked at me now with questions etched on their faces.

"What, no good?" Johnny asked.

"How bad is it?" Sheri translated.

"Well, we've got a lot of work ahead of us and we're gonna need more dumpsters. It's a nightmare down there. This whole thing has got to go" I said, waving my arm around the room.

"Should have known it wouldn't be simple with everything else we've seen here," Sheri said.

"Yeah," I replied, "but this is huge."

"Eh, no worries, Kawika, we get 'em." John was already pulling out the saws and cords.

Sheri and I glanced at each other, both knowing how lucky we were to find him, and turned back to what we were doing. She continued to haul out debris, while John and I began to cut out the floor, piece by piece.

"Well, Rod's gonna be surprised," I said as we went back to work.

Rod and his wife Sally had been friends with my parents for as long as I can remember, but it wasn't until my early twenties that I got to know him myself. It was 1991 and my first house was in need of a new roof. At the time, computers were gaining in popularity, but if there was an internet, I knew nothing about it. I was reading construction books trying to figure out how to do this thing myself, without hiring a contractor.

I brought it up to my dad while we were tinkering around at the shop one day and, of course, he said he knew someone. He said he bowled and played golf with a guy named Rod, and asked me if I remembered him. I said I didn't think so. My father went on to explain that Rod has a small contracting business, and owed my dad a favor. He said if I was willing to help, I could probably get it done for only the cost of shingles.

Hard to turn that down. My dad had a knack for collecting a lot of friends, a few long-time. Some were close. Most were people he had done some plumbing job or another for and kept them around for whatever future service he might need. Maybe a walkway at the house poured, or a bowling ball re-drilled. He lived in a world of traded services, and it seems he was quietly trying to show me his mastery of the game. There would be a return on my part, some future obligation to be met, favors paid with favors. I'm sure a plumbing job that required free labor loomed in my future. I thought of it as the redneck mafia, "you owe me one rolling of my lawn and it's time to pay up." Of course, I was happy to return the goodwill, to me it was only human. I had to laugh to myself at my dad's whole backroom, cloak and dagger style.

Rod and I spent two days up there, tearing off old roofing, rolling out new paper, and finally re-shingling. We got to know each other a little bit. When he joined us on the first day, I was able to put a face with the name, and yes, I did know him. At well over six feet, he was an imposing figure, with a voice that got your attention, and his point across. If he thought you were bullshitting him, he wouldn't hesitate to call you on it. He was this big, intimidating cover, wrapped around a person who would completely rearrange his schedule if he knew you needed him. All this I learned on my own later, as our relationship grew.

From that first day, Rod treated me like an adult, tossing me beers and jabs up on that roof like I was one of his crew. I felt good, older somehow, and even though my dad was always there, hovering, I felt comfortable.

Years later, on the day my mother died, it wasn't surprising to see him, and out of all my parent's friends, only him, waiting with my dad at the hospital when I arrived early in the morning. When that horrible, final moment finally came, and Rod saw my face crumble, he wrapped me up in a bear hug for what seemed an eternity, and I was grateful. He then did the same to Sheri.

It was something my father couldn't bring himself to do, not then, not ever. There were one-armed embraces for sure, and plenty of tears on my part, but he remained stoic and showed absolutely no emotion. Our encounters together since that day have been filled with an unspoken void.

Rod, Sally, Sheri, and I, grew closer on that day and through the years that followed so that when we moved to Kauai, they assured us that they would be among the first to visit. He asked me once if I was running from, or to. The question was so direct that it caught me off guard. I said to, of course. I want to chase something, even if I don't know what it is yet. He looked at me, skeptical and knowing. I guess the truth is, it's a lot of both.

I don't know what agencies were at work around us, but whether it was some benevolent force like good karma, good fortune, or good luck, is still up for debate. It could be something altogether different, like good timing, or just simple coincidence. I know we weren't walking on water, so the answer is not likely in that direction, but call it what you will, it was on our side. Solutions to issues, big or small, would land at our feet within days, sometimes hours, of their discovered need. Answers to lingering questions were given voice in unexpected places as if they had drifted out of thin air.

I found a great electrician while buying a drill on Craig's List. After making the transaction, I asked him if he knew anyone who could do some electrical work, he introduced me to his cousin, who ended up re-wiring the whole restaurant. We continued to have all these generally common experiences that just seemed to fall into place, the right thing at the right time so to speak, so when the phone rang at their house, Rod and Sally were unknowingly only moments away from being sucked into the vortex.

We had been in touch with them since we moved, and they were talking about coming to Kauai sometime in April. Maybe. Sally was the owner of a small-town ice cream store that didn't open until the end of May, and Rod just finished an addition and was waiting for the ground to thaw. They outlined all this for us as they considered a late April or early May visit. A perfectly logical conversation, sane even, way back in November, or December, but now I was hoping to move the date up a little. Perhaps even risk shading the conversation with a touch of lunacy.

We called him on the morning of March third, after we had been working on the space for two days, and getting a handle on what we were going to do. The conversation was long, as exchanges with Rod often are, and we filled him in on what we had taken over, and the condition it was in. I told him that I really wished he were standing next to me right now because I could use his help on a big tile project that seems to be priority one.

He laughed like maybe he thought I was joking, and said he'd be happy to help any way he can, and I knew it to be the truth because I had walked down that road with him many times before. We went back and forth about life here, and winter there, what our plan for the restaurant was, and how his summer schedule was shaping up. I was picking around the edges of what I wanted to come out and say, and I wasn't even sure how to approach it. I tried asking him questions about the project that was in front of us, but I couldn't think of any. Besides, it seemed pointless, I needed more than just to pick his brain, I needed him to see what I was seeing.

"You know what, Rod. Why don't you just come out here now, I'll pay for your plane tickets, and we'll call it a working vacation. You said yourself that you're spinning your wheels for the next couple of months, and from what you just described out your window, it sounds like you could use some tropical sunshine. I don't say this often, and some would say not nearly enough, but I need you. The sooner the better.

"You sound pretty serious, and you don't need to pay for our tickets, David. We already talked about April sometime, maybe early May, we just haven't looked at the calendar yet to set a date."

"Covering your airfare has already been decided Rod, believe me, it's the least we can do for what I'm asking, and you're staying with us. We can show you the island, do a little work, drink some beers, and you can forget about winter for a while. What is it, ten degrees?"

"No, it's twenty." He said, laughing.

"Well, I was hoping you'd like to trade it for Kauai, immediately. I don't want to sound desperate, or abrupt, but we have taken on quite a bite here, it's a lot to chew and digest, and frankly, I'm in the dark. Can you guys come? will you?" I pleaded.

I didn't realize how homesick I was for the people we left behind, but now with the prospect of our first visitor, I was like Molly and that damn tennis ball. Rod, since my mother's death, had become a kind of lifeline for me, allowing me to connect to someone else who was also close to her. He's the type of guy who earns your respect quickly, as he did for Sheri, having known him only a short time. Despite our age difference and the fact that he knew me as a kid, although he never once treated me that way, we developed our own friendship late in life. However, I still don't think he was entirely grasping the idea that we needed him now, like right now.

"I'll talk to Sally, see if we can put together some dates, and let you know. She opens the store in May, so we're pretty free till then. I expect April, rather than May." He said in his slow drawl.

"How about the seventh." I countered.

"April seventh might work; what day is that."

"Honestly, Rod, I don't know anybody here, I don't know who I can trust, I don't even know what I'm getting into. You would bring peace of mind and a lot of stability to this situation. I was hoping for March seventh. I'll e-mail you the tickets. Please." There was silence on the line.

"Hello? Hello?" I said.

"Sorry, I dropped my phone trying to turn the volume up, I thought you said *March* seven, as in later this week." He said, confused.

"I did. I know it's soon."

"*Soon*, hell David, summer's coming *soon*, this is more like yesterday." There was humor in his voice, so I knew he was quietly getting excited about the suddenness of my request.

"I know, it's crazy, but if you guys can just get here, we'll take care of everything. It would mean a lot if you two were part of building this dream."

"I hear it in your voice, we'll make it work, I'll talk to Sally and re-arrange a couple of things, we'll make it work."

Sally was thrilled, and more than willing to do this on the spur of the moment. She clearly had no idea what she was getting into. When they agreed, later in the day, we had plane tickets already waiting for them in their e-mail. Rod was under the impression that he had some tile work and grouting that would be his main focus, mostly because that's what I told him. What I neglected to mention in conversations before they arrived, was how big the flooring project was growing.

By the time they landed, Johnny, Sheri, and I had removed every sign that any floor had ever existed, save for the three-foot deep hole that encompassed a twenty-foot by thirty-foot area, and a couple of random beams. We were hauling out so much rotted, and crumbling wood that, for a while, we were swapping dumpsters every other day.

"Holy shit, David, what have you gotten yourselves into? It looks like a hell of a lot more than some tile work." His whole statement was said while somehow laughing.

"Yeah, it's kind of grown over the last few days. I figured you needed to see it for yourself. No words can explain this, am I right?" I said.

"You are certainly right. Well, no sense in standing around, I've got three weeks to see what we can do, might just as well make a material list."

The next day we rented a truck and filled it with all the lumber we would need, along with enough screws, nails, and other hardware to supply a small army of carpenters, which is essentially what I had assembled. We built our friendship, the five of us, while we began to put this damn restaurant back together. It was a mess that we were slowly organizing and re-creating. Turning it back into what it was meant to be after it had been neglected for so long, and left in such a repugnant state. Rod and Sally were tireless as we all continued to move from one thing to the next.

Johnny became Rod's go-to when it came to boards cut to the right length, a show of respect that he wore proudly. We had set aside plenty of time for them to enjoy a Hawaiian vacation, see the island and do the touristy thing, which they did to some extent. But all Rod wanted to do was work, said he was happiest when he was working, so we let him.

By the time we hugged for the last time and said our grateful, and heartfelt goodbyes, we had again secured promises of a return visit. We had begun to transform the entire restaurant, literally from the ground up. In the three weeks that they were here, Johnnylove, Rod, and I rebuilt the entire floor under what would be the service, prep, bar, and kitchen area. New posts, beams, floor joists, plywood decking, and cement board, finally gave way to new commercial tile, which arrived a scant four days before they were leaving.

Meanwhile, the girls were busy power washing the floors in the two covered lanai's that served as the dining rooms, and from there they moved on to staining and sealing them. After that, they went about cleaning and painting each room, and continued to haul out debris that was still being created. Somebody, it seemed, was constantly sweeping.

We always had a few ice-cold longnecks when the day ended. It was a celebration of unwinding after work, known in the islands as pau hana. We would toast each other for what we accomplished that day. We raised our bottles for life and prosperity on Kauai, we hailed our friendship, and at times we reminisced about my mother. Rod and Sally knew her so well that it was like she was there with us. On those occasions, I would squirrel away the bottle caps for a thought that I had stuck on the back burner.

We'll never forget what Rod and Sally did for us, and they're agreeing to show up in Kauai from Michigan, with an absurd four-day notice, was only the beginning. They brought a feeling of home, and family, and when they were gone, he had left us with a foundation for our future.

## CHAPTER 11

# The dream emerges

Throughout that hot, often windless summer, we tore out every inch of electrical wire, drywall, and plumbing that the space contained, and started from the beginning. Johnny would pull down ceilings and walls leaving only the studs, and Sheri and I would come along behind sweeping and hauling out drywall debris and marking the boards that needed replacing.

When the hard labor of the day was over, we'd sprint home for a shower and then spend most of the evening trying to figure out the day-to-day of operating a restaurant. The hands-on, the re-building, the plumbing, hell even the decorating and final appointments, those things were in my wheelhouse, my comfort zone, but this, this was something else.

It was a summer-long crash course in not just restaurant management, but restaurant ownership. We spent a lot of time educating ourselves about the procedures, and practices of operating a successful business, and the more we learned and began to grasp, the less stressful it became. Without going into profit margins, product loss, or cost overruns, I can honestly say that common sense, and a willingness to learn were the main ingredients.

YouTube was burning up the battery life on my I-phone. We poured through food safety and proper food handling resources, the Hawaiian health code, and articles on how to set up a commercial kitchen. We learned and memorized the liquor laws and prepared for licensing. Sheri researched the business side of things, like learning the laws about tipped employees and wage guidelines or setting up the accounting, payroll, and taxes.

We bounced ideas, theories, procedures, and things we had read, or seen off each other all the time. It was the scariest, most thrilling part. The thought of throwing our doors wide open to the public and laying ourselves bare was as terrifying as it was alluring. We had overcome a lot just to get to this point and this was just another hurdle to be scaled, one of the few to this point that we could see down the track and measure.

So, throughout our summer of construction and preparation, we had so many balls up in the air that I felt like a circus juggler auditioning for Barnum and Bailey. We re-wired the whole place from the new fuse box to the farthest outlet. I replaced all the plumbing from outside to the last sink. We were drywalling and securing rows of shelving. The kitchen walls were being covered in sheets of stainless steel, and Johnny and I were installing the large walk-in cooler and setting the compressor.

The bar itself angled around a center post to create a ninety-degree turn and seated about fifteen people. With its beaten and tired surface, the structure was out of place in front of the newly tiled floor. We knew from the beginning that the whole thing would need to be replaced, but when I took a few kicks at the rotted, pieced-together half wall, that somehow managed to support the counter, it collapsed with an ease even the French would find appalling.

I re-built the L-shaped bar wall the next day and before I covered the studs with drywall, I carefully attached the bottle caps I had saved for my mom. I left a note for her behind one of the water pipes so that someday, someone will know we had been there and why. Later, we dropped in custom bar tops that were designed to mimic the ancient longboards of the past and covered them with a hard, clear epoxy. Now my mom has a place at my bar.

Through it all Sheri was working on décor. Imagining unique ideas, and incorporating bits of the island. While some of these projects proved rather difficult to construct or install, or in some cases even move, they gave our restaurant a personal touch and a sense of verity, and together it all began to form a theme, a walk back in time. Johnny and I somehow managed to keep everything in one piece.

As we installed the three glass murals depicting the basic elements of what we were representing in our menu, land, sea, and fire, which commanded your attention along the hallway at the entrance, she had already begun on a large work that would hang above the opening to the back dining room. The mosaic would feature the lush green, and mountainous backdrop of Koloa, including the ancient sugar mill. All of it was produced from broken and scattered tiles in a multitude of colors that we were given permission to collect from the bungalows of Kauai's fabled and now crumbling Coco Palms Resort.

Our house, back in Michigan, was an exhibit in stained glass and mosaics that Sheri had created over the years. We had elephants, cranes, cattails, lakes, swans, and fish, all on display and making every room brighter, from the basement bar top to the glass on the wine room door to the high windows in the family room and entryway. Each piece of glass was hand-cut and arranged perfectly. She re-created the entire Mackinaw Bridge at sunset spanning four tall side windows of our garage. It was stunning.

Aside from the tile that we had collected from the Coco Palms, Bamboo is what we really wanted, as much as we could get and everywhere possible. I wanted the look of a tiki hut and the feel of the tropics. We wanted, for the time you spent in our restaurant, to take you to a different place, maybe even a different time. Our goal was to create a certain atmosphere and a seduction so that from the moment you crossed the threshold of our door, you were on Hawaiian time. I could visualize the feeling, but without a name for the restaurant, I was having trouble seeing the overall theme.

So, Sheri and I started to really think about it. We spent a few evenings down on the rocks below our condo talking about the islands and what they represented. We tried to list all the things that made them unique to so many people. Hawaii was at one time its own sovereign nation long before it became America's fiftieth state, carrying forward a Polynesian culture that went back a thousand years or more. We wanted our name to reflect more than just a cliched reference to a tropical sunset or an ocean breeze, and instead showcase who we are and what we want.

We knew what our menu was going to look like, we knew what kind of food we were going to serve, and what we wanted the atmosphere to feel like. For a long time, we had kicked around one name after another for our restaurant and couldn't seem to settle on one that felt right. With all the lush vegetation and tropical foliage that gave this island its nickname, it turned out that we only had to stand quietly and look around at the space we were creating, at the very heart of the vision we wanted, and what we wanted was

Kauai, and so from then on, our restaurant became The Garden Island Grille.

With our name established, and the ideas for the look and feel of the place coming together, we set out to find someone who could put those visions into colorful signage. Something that would capture not only the attention of our guests but also hint at the experience they would find, once inside. When our search concluded, we knew we had found the right guy.

We met Tommy Cook after mentioning to a friend that we had no idea where to find a quality sign maker. Our friend owned the ice cream shop in town and Tommy had done all his creative artwork. He passed along my number and Tommy called me the next day to set up a meeting. His ideas from the beginning and the examples he showed us were second to none, and I could see that this was going to be a good relationship.

It was on one of these visits to go over the final details on signage that he brought with him an eight-foot piece of black bamboo as big around as my thigh. It was lacquered and polished and seemed to glow as he carried it on his shoulder. After setting it on the floor he announced that he had found it in his storage shed, and after cleaning it up he thought we might like to have it. We knew how rare black bamboo was, so we didn't hesitate in showing our appreciation.

With his actual purpose for the visit forgotten, which usually happens, we talked about our ideas for the look of the place, the feel we wanted, and the vibe we were hoping to create. Of course, our focus centered on bamboo, and lots of it. Where we'd put it, how we'd use it, and finally where we'd find it, filled the hour we found ourselves lost in.

Tommy said he had a patch of bamboo on his property that was growing out of control and would be glad to give us as much as we wanted, as long as we came up to his place in Lawai and hacked it down. A couple of beers, and several thank-you's, were passed around and we set a date to fire up some chainsaws. Tommy left, having never even approached the reason for his drop-in, yet we accomplished so much more.

Shortly after, we were gathered in the driveway overlooking his expansive property, our feet clad in sensible hiking shoes and carrying a couple of machetes, trying to pinpoint the bamboo. Tommy provided the chainsaw. While we worked through a Becks that he pulled from a cooler, he showed us the house and the various projects he had going on around it. We walked through his wife's gardens, took a tour of the one-room workshop that he labeled 'World Headquarters', and finally came to a thick rope that marked the beginning of our small adventure.

The rope extended some forty yards down a steep slope to a level path about three feet wide. That's where the rope ended, the hill continued down another fifty yards, through trees I couldn't name and some kind of menacing ground cover, to the road below. A hundred feet down the path, situated on a vertical down slope, stood a wide circle of bamboo, their hollow trunks knocking together like the rattle of bones, bringing an eeriness to this bizarre trek.

I lingered at the top, wondering how we'd get the bamboo up the slope once we cut it, and figured Tommy had a plan. Pulled from my musings, I discovered that he and Johnny had already started repelling down the hill, gripping the rope to keep their footing, and were nearing the bottom. I shrugged, looked at Sheri, and swung over the edge.

As I reached the halfway point, I began keeping an eye out for Sherpas to lend a hand, it was that far removed from ordinary. After descending to the end of the rope, we gathered on the narrow path. Sheri was a coiled spring of excitement; she was practically vibrating. She announced to no one in particular that this was amazing. The whole thing gave new meaning to the phrase 'shopping adventure.'

We spent two hours liberating bamboo and sliding it the rest of the way down the hill to the road below. That turned out to be the obvious solution rather than hauling it up, and one that worked perfectly. Johnny was wielding the chainsaw, and the rest of us were whacking off branches with machetes and launching the heavy poles down to the road below.

A gentle slope further along the path beyond the bamboo led us around the house to a long stairway ascending toward the driveway. I turned my head, and with a smile, shot a quizzical look at Tommy. He shrugged without remorse and said he thought the rope would be more fun, add to the adventure, a story to go with the ambiance. I slapped him on the shoulder and said I couldn't agree more.

A few weeks later we found ourselves staring at a hand-lettered sign reading 'estate sale,' with an arrow pointing toward a narrow lane. We turned in and after a couple of bends found a rather large two-story house, ringed by palm trees and a spacious open yard. Parked off to one side was what looked like a glorified eight-passenger golf cart that had collided with a thatched roof hut. It was awesome. Bent over it was a fifty-something man in jeans and a rolled-up flannel shirt. He appeared to be tinkering with the engine.

We made our introductions, and he said his name was Doug. He told us that he owned and drove the Aloha Shuttle, throwing a thumb over his shoulder indicating the little grass shack on wheels. Poipu's limousine for sunset excursions, south shore bar hopping, and late-night revelry, he claimed. All with no charge. Tips only, and he was expanding. We were impressed.

We told him we were opening up a restaurant in Koloa and we were looking for something unique, but we didn't know what it was. We'd know when we found it though. He nodded his head slowly in stoic agreement. He seemed to understand what we were talking about as if he had also been on that search at one time or another. Sheri and I were drawn to this man instantly. There was some kind of kindred spirit like with Tommy, and Johnnylove that brought us together.

He led us to a door and told us to go ahead and look around the house, that he'd catch up with us in a bit. He went back to pack up whatever he was doing, and we were left to wander a stranger's house alone. Weird. But at the same time kind of interesting, peeking behind the curtain of someone else's life. We were picking up, and eyeing suspiciously, relics that once meant so much to someone. Sometimes wondering why.

Everything was for sale, from the furniture to the appliances. Lots of artwork and table items, knick-knacks of high quality, stuff here, stuff there, that kind of thing. We picked up something only to put it down later, picked up something else, then traded it for another, and again set that down. There was a lot of interesting stuff at this estate sale, just nothing that said I belong in your restaurant. Meanwhile, Doug appeared out of nowhere and said he had something to show us.

Down an outside stairway, we went to a covered patio below. Under a tarp, which he pulled back with a flourish, were two intricately carved and deeply polished tikis, made from the trunk of a large tree. They had the look of being cleaved from the same stout log, like twins, but different in their own subtle ways. We were immediately captivated. Our eyes were unable to be drawn away from the two statues that stood before us. Without saying a word to each other, we both knew that this is what we had come for.

Doug was possibly a full two minutes into his known history of what we were looking at before I even realized he was talking. I looked at him blinking, trying not to give away the fact that I hadn't heard a damn word of what he just said. Instead, I elbowed Sheri out of her daze and told him that we wanted them. This is what we were looking for. We already knew exactly where they would go.

He said if we wanted them that he'd be happy to donate them to the restaurant, but he wouldn't take any money for them. I was a little uncomfortable loading them into the Jeep, even though he steadfastly refused any offer I pushed at him. I noticed that he had a tree service digging up a few trees that dotted the landscape. I talked him into a cash deal to move one of the small palms to the courtyard of the restaurant. Now, I finally have my very own palm tree, planted deep and growing strong, right next to what would become the Aloha Stage at the Garden Island Grille.

We stationed the two tikis inside the front entrance, quietly guarding each side of the short hallway leading into the restaurant, their maniacal faces greeting anyone who entered and promising a unique experience. I stepped back to again check their alignment after mounting them to the floor when I noticed Johnny, who was standing across the hall from me. He kept looking back and forth from one to the next as if he were watching ping-pong and blinking like a high-speed shutter on a Pentax.

"What's wrong with you?" I said. "What, you don't like them?"

"Don't know, they feel funny, where you gettum?" He asked.

"I told you, an estate sale, the guy who drives the Aloha Shuttle, he's moving, said he's had 'em a while." I offered.

"Where he gettum? I mean eh, where they come from first, who gettum before these guys?" I didn't understand why he seemed so suddenly alarmed.

"Why, what's wrong with them, I don't get it, why are you being so weird?"

"If you don't know the beginning of who gettum first, what was in the mind of the man who carved them, then you don't know why they were made, or what they were made for. We need to pray; we need a blessing on these." He said as he began calling everyone to gather in the front.

"Okay, everyone, hold hands, we're gonna pray for these guys." He said. A rough circle formed under a dim light just inside the open front doors.

It was Sheri, me, some dude named Brandon that helped out once in a while, Raul, my electrician, and finally Johnny, the guy who called the meeting, all standing in a prayer circle at eight o'clock on a breathless summer night, holding hands and staring at our shoes. Johnny drank plenty, but he also liked to pray a lot, hold hands and pray. It's how he was raised, I guess. We had to shut him down sometimes when he'd had way too much to drink because it just didn't seem right, drunk praying. But he was a believer.

He began in earnest with an array of thank-you's that sounded like an academy speech and I was starting to wonder if he had gotten off track, it was sounding like his safe travels prayer that often ended our time together. Suddenly he turned and laid both hands on each tiki, one after the other, and spoke words of blessing. He prayed that each would be a totem of peace, and a guardian of life and property.

He then bellowed, with Moses-like authority, something I will never forget, and still chills me today. It wasn't so much what he said, but the power with which he conveyed the message, and it was haunting.

"Whatever was in the mind of your maker, whatever intent resides in this wood, you do not belong here. This is a new place and I command you by the power of God to get out, flee, and be gone, and may the grace of the almighty fill the void."

I've mentioned before that I'm not a spiritual person, not a churchgoer if you will, nor is Sheri for that matter. But I do believe in some kind of greater power, I'm just not sure I'm ready, or even able to define it. Religion and politics are two things I stay away from, I have found no answers in either. That being said, I am also not a conspiracy buff, ancient astronaut theorist, or ghost hunter, so what I tell you here I have no theory toward or understanding of.

As we all stood there, shocked by the loud outburst from Johnny, a cold wind rushed past us, ruffling our shirts, blowing our hair, and raising goose flesh in its wake as it raced by. It flew down the hall in a scurry of dust and paper, slamming both doors as it departed. That was the feeling we were all left with. Something had swept out, and not so gently. Whatever it was, it caused the doors to slam themselves closed in its wake. This rush of air originated within the confined space of the restaurant, where no wind could ever come from, it directed itself toward the tikis, and the blast it delivered was arctic.

Hands were gripped tighter and heads snapped up looking around in confusion. In that moment before everyone started talking at once, in that fraction of time before anyone found their voice, I saw Raul, who I guess was Catholic, crossing himself fervently. I saw Brandon jump away from the tiki he was standing next to, shooting a look at the back door for his escape, as though it may suddenly come alive and give chase. And I saw Johnnylove, his face a mask of astonishment, and his eyes as wide as Texas, unblinking.

Johnny mumbled amen at the same instant everyone reclaimed themselves and began tumbling words all over the place, tripping over each other's exclamations, and inquisitions. Everyone was babbling all at once. Everything being said boiled down to one thing. What the hell just happened?

No one knew. Most of us sat around for another hour offering up explanations, telling stories of other weird experiences, although none as weird as this, and giving our own philosophies and views. Including Johnny, who would only hold to his biblical theories. But in the end, no one really could answer the question of what the hell just happened, and eventually, we just stopped asking. It became part of the lore of the Garden Island Grille.

## CHAPTER 12

# Anxiety, fear, and the big Hawaiian

With the remodel and re-design of the restaurant finished, and with all of our equipment in place, we were now waiting on the county to complete inspections and give us the thumbs up to open. We had split, cut, and trimmed Tommy's bamboo, and turned the entire restaurant into a veritable tiki hut. With the look of thatch falling over the roof edge, the feel was complete. Bamboo served almost every possible function. Masking corners, covering headers, framing pictures and doorways, and making up chair rails. It even covered entire walls in some places.

We appointed the back-bar area with a few swanky neon signs, a huge Kona Brewing surfboard, tributes to old Hawaii, and memories from a past life lived so many miles, and what felt like a lifetime away. Michigan seemed untethered in our minds, every day floating farther and farther behind us, while ahead was a horizon awash with possibilities.

An array of tables make up the open air, covered lanais on either side of the bar, and each room carries its own theme. The back is devoted to the wealth of movies that were filmed here on

Kauai. It features a kaleidoscope of candid snapshots and cinema premiers, rare behind-the-scenes photographs, and the movie stars that touched our island. Sprinkled among the celebrities that enshroud an entire wall, is a cast of residents from around the island who found a few minutes of fame in the role of extras. If you look hard enough, you'll encounter Johnny Depp with his arm around some guy from Waimea, or Spielberg caught in an animated wave as he instructs a group of locals on the art of running from a dinosaur. It's a montage of almost every movie filmed on Kauai, and it showcases why Hollywood finds this island so attractive.

Spending as much time here as he did, Elvis Presley is well remembered, and well represented on that back wall. After the filming of Blue Hawaii, in which the wedding scene encompassed much of the grounds of the beautiful Coco Palms hotel, he fell in love with the resort, returning over and over through the late fifties and sixties.

Elvis had already become a worldwide superstar, but he would still roll into the Coco Palms handing out his version of aloha, and wandering the grounds like everyone else. Guests would find him bussing tables in the main dining room, chatting amiably with the Hawaiian roasting the pig on the outdoor spit, or casually strolling the lagoons, all in an attempt to blend in, if not for a little while. The pull of the spotlight was too strong to resist, however, and the King would grab an ukulele and sit in with the band that was playing the cocktail lounge, or the Flame room, or the Coconut Palace, and bring the small house down. What a time it must have been.

With the memories of the near past safely secured in photographs, and artfully displayed throughout the back of our restaurant, with some of its contents spilling into the lounge area around the bar, we head toward the entrance, and oddly enough, further back in time. The front is a more intimate feeling, closer to the stage with most of the tables situated for two. In the evening, with darkness settling in, the lighting is scant and cozy.

The lone wall in this open, airy and comfortable room, is home to a selection of stories, chants, traditions, photographs, and paintings of ancient Hawaii and the royalty that once ruled it. Inside the small courtyard, finch, cardinal, and mynah birds come and go among the heliconia, elephant's ear, bougainvillea, lime, papaya, and the dozens of ferns that surround a music stage I was building almost entirely out of bamboo.

As the summer was nearing its end we had very little left to do before we were ready to open. We were anticipating sometime in September, but no date had been firmly set. The anxiety I was feeling was long past simple nerves and redlining toward a breakdown. While we waited, we spent a lot of time talking about each area of the restaurant. It just fell into place more than it was decided, that I would hire and manage the cooks, prep, dishwashers, and everything else that concerned the kitchen, including the product ordering. Sheri took up the task of hiring and managing the servers, host staff, bartenders, and all the bar stock that came with that job.

We were slowly developing our roles, dividing and fine-tuning the aspects of the restaurant that we would handle separately. It was the kitchen that would be my biggest role and to this point, my greatest fear. I had formed a vague plan and that seemed to scare me more than having no plan at all. I figured if I thought I had any knowledge of what I was attempting to do, I was only fooling myself.

I admit that beneath the surface of an otherwise calm exterior, was a man terrified of opening his business. I knew Sheri was too. We spent very little time airing our fears to each other, there were always more important things to consider. Whether it was learning the health code, memorizing the liquor law, or finding the right salt and pepper shakers, we kept our minds looking forward. Giving fear a voice is a deterrent to that goal. We sometimes poked around the edges of what truly scared us, but we figured those things would eventually take care of themselves.

As we looked ahead to the county's approval, those fears had moved to the front of the line, and with so little to occupy us, they were creeping into all of our conversations. We finally let them have their say one night and discovered that most of what we feared was common, open-a-business kind of stuff. Will we have any customers? Will they want to come back? What will they think of the food? Do my employees know what they're doing? Do I know what I'm doing? Can we pay the bills? A laundry list of concerns and worries that would solve themselves once we started doing business. But that was the problem. We had no idea when that was going to happen, which meant that all these considerations for the mind would continue uninterrupted. A constant stream of abuse, and insolence, like dealing with my own middle-aged bully.

Getting those things off our mind's allowed us to look at them differently and realize that they weren't worth worrying about. I discovered that by getting our trepidations out into the open and vocalizing all the things that were freaking us out, the road ahead seemed to have fewer hairpin turns, and things didn't look so scary.

The one item that stood out was the kitchen. We both knew how to cook, and we could make our entire menu, of course, but this was a different animal. There was so much more to it than what my mind would allow me to see, which was essentially just simply firing up a burner, and whipping something up for the family. That's why I was so terrified, the magnitude of it all. It was something no book could ever teach, or series on YouTube could ever prepare you for. Unfortunately, only experience could do that, and that was one thing we had yet to acquire.

It was our own best-kept secret that Sheri and I had absolutely no knowledge or work history in the business we were trying to build, the restaurant that was taking shape around us. It's not for a lack of respect. Or an idea that it's so easy anyone can do it, or anything remotely resembling arrogance that led us in this direction. We simply had a passionate desire to do this, and when the opportunity was dangled in front of us, like a well-cut ribeye, we snapped it up.

Of course, It's been brought to our attention more than once, that the failure rate within the first year of such an endeavor was well over sixty percent and skyrocketed to eighty within five years, so the whole thing was madness. A potential fool's dream that could only rob us of everything. But honestly, it didn't matter. We wanted this. Asked for it even. Poked it from the shadows of our minds, and pursued it into the light. We needed the challenge. The new lifestyle we were now living was requiring more and more for us to reach beyond anything that we thought we could do, tapping internal resources that we didn't know we had, or re-testing ones that had proven faulty in the past.

So, the kitchen was the basis of all our fears as it turned out. Mine anyway. Every little item that brought anxiety rushing to the surface was magnified by one thing. The kitchen. It would be the workhorse of the restaurant, the solid core that all the other parts revolved around, and I was under a lot of pressure to get it right.

Everyone I talked to about it said all I needed was a chef as if the mere mention of the word should settle any debate. A chef, case closed. But, did we really need a chef? After all, the menu was set, and the recipes were thoroughly vetted and approved. The more I broke down the menu and took a hard look at it, the more I realized that what I needed was a damn good prep guy. I also realized that while a chef, in traditional terms, was not the answer, there was still something I needed. I just wasn't sure exactly what that was.

What was going through my mind in terms of a preferred solution, I thought was too much to ask for. It felt like I was pressing my luck. What it boiled down to was finding someone who not only excelled as an hourly line cook, but also had the ability to teach me the ins and outs, and the day-to-day operation of a commercial kitchen. The problem was actually bigger than that. The reality of our situation was that the restaurant seating was more than the tiny cooking area could ever possibly serve.

Somewhere in the past life of the restaurant, someone had taken the liberty of removing a dividing wall that housed an unused office and created a second dining room. Although the seating capacity had doubled in size, the kitchen remained the same small, crowded place that it had always been. And because of the complicated building codes, that could not be changed. So, we knew that coordinating the organization as the food moved from cooking to plating, and on to the table, was essential to our success.

We needed someone who was more than just a cook and a part of our growing family but also had the experience to understand the menu, recognize the restrictions in the size of our kitchen, and create a sensible, and efficient flow to the line. To date, I had found no one who came even close to matching that description. I wasn't sure what I was going to do.

Johnny and I were in the courtyard one afternoon, erecting giant bamboo poles and sweating in the sun. The thick, stout columns would eventually hold up the thatched roof of the Aloha Stage. I was standing on a ladder trying to pound a bamboo cross-beam into a bamboo post like I'm prehistoric man or something when in walked the biggest Hawaiian we had met so far. It wasn't so much his physical size, although he was every bit intimidating. He just had this natural way of filling the room with his presence. We seemed to move toward him as if he held his own gravity, our feet walking of their own accord until by some miracle, Sheri and I were standing directly in front of him. Johnny was still wandering around the stage, unaffected.

As we stood there gawking, he made a few comments and reeled off a few questions pertaining to what we were doing, and we told him our intentions. He said he had heard that someone was planning to open where the old Tomcats was located and wanted to check it out. The restaurant that once occupied this space, and had over the months given us so much grief, had earned itself a very jaded and seedy reputation around the south end. Its beaten and tired appearance was mostly the result of simple neglect and late-night parties. It spoke to blowouts that wandered into the small hours and included too much alcohol, too many fights, and too little common sense, all mingling with the echo and distortion of some live and loud cover band. It had all taken its toll, not only on the building, but in the community that surrounded it.

That was not our intended plan, and certainly not the illusion we had crafted in our minds for the restaurant, so we quickly erased those ideas when we told him this would be nothing like Tomcats. He seemed satisfied with that and continued ambling around the now vacant space, temporarily lost in another time. Meanwhile, we made our introductions. He said his name was Robert, and I offered him a Heineken. As we stood there shuffling our feet and drinking our beers, he shared a bit about himself.

He told us that his last name, Kanahele, was one of the oldest names in Hawaii. His family was originally from Niihau, an island visible off the western shore of Kauai, where a handful of pure Hawaiians make their life and all others are forbidden. His quick sense of humor had us all laughing almost immediately. He said he worked in this spot ten or twelve years ago, when it was another restaurant, and went on to regale us with stories of his youth and growing up on Kauai.

He continued to return day after day, always with mounting enthusiasm, shaking his head in disbelief at what we had turned the place into, and how we had brought it back to life. Robert revealed more and more of himself and he, in turn, learned a lot about who we were. The friendship was instant and lasting, although for reasons beyond our control, it would not remain as close as it was in the beginning.

He volunteered to lend a hand and it was while he was working with Johnny and me, finishing the roof on the bamboo stage, that we discovered he was a chef at the Hyatt in Poipu. That perked my ears up. With surprise at what I was hearing, I fired off questions without thinking just to keep him on the subject. I was compelled to find out what he knew, how he knew it, and how far that knowledge ran. But most importantly, I needed to know if he wanted another job.

For months I had been anguishing over the kitchen and how it would run. The overall, day-to-day business of the restaurant didn't scare me as much as it once did. Don't get me wrong, my nerves were as frayed as a hippie's poncho, but I figured most of this was just teaching, challenging, and managing people, and Sheri and

I could figure that out. The kitchen, however, the lifeblood of the restaurant, for some reason was a black hole in my mind.

I could picture how I wanted it done. I knew how everything was made and the process it took. I just could not seem to put it all together in a cohesive and convenient way. I understood what the cooks would need immediately in front of them to cook and plate the menu. I lacked knowledge on how to set that up and build a system. It would get done, even if I had to muddle through a few months of on-the-fly changes, but basically, I was stymied.

We couldn't have known then, when Robert first walked through the front doors and down the short hallway, that we would gain a friend that would pour his heart and energy into us and his passion into the restaurant. A man that openly shared his life and the stories that went with it, and who, through the coming months, would set ablaze with the light of a thousand suns the darkness that had so mystified me.

Almost from the beginning, he became our uninvested third partner, and that's exactly how we treated him. No meeting, big or small, ever took place without the three of us presenting as one. He took from my hands the arrangement and set up of the kitchen, the hot and cold line, and what, how, and who to order from. He began making list after list of cooking utensils, wire whips, pots, pans, mixing bowls, containers, and other items we still needed. Slowly, I was learning all the things that were left previously unknown, the fear was melting away, and in its place, a newfound certainty was taking shape.

By the time we had met Robert, we had acquired all the appliances and furnishings it would take to set up the whole place. Our detailed lists included everything needed to outfit a full bar, kitchen, dish room, prep area, serving station, and two dining rooms. We had spent a good deal of time sifting through endless online catalogues looking at everything from draught dispensers, dining room tables, and walk-in coolers, to ice makers, fryers, grills, and sinks. It took a while to finalize a list that filled two containers and have it shipped to Kauai from California, but when I had finally started building the stage, we had put together every table and chair, connected every sink, and turned an empty space into a fully functioning restaurant.

It was during that time that we began setting up local suppliers. We developed a relationship with a rancher for the beef, partnered with the farming program at the community college to provide some of the vegetables, and found people who grew fruits, coconuts, vanilla, lemongrass, and herbs. We connected with boat captains to bring us the best fish. We purchased Kauai shrimp that was brought fresh to our door, and we met a guy who grew only oyster mushrooms and delivered them himself. The island provided a unique opportunity to be literally a farm-to-table restaurant in nearly every manner. We even bought locally-made coconut ice cream for the pina coladas, as well as rum distilled less than a mile away.

Robert was easily able to work with the equipment that we had, re-arranging some of it from the way I had placed everything, admiring the gleaming stainless, and vowing to keep it that way. He was proud and full of confidence, but he also knew the value of what he was looking at. Not what each piece had cost me, but what the equipment that surrounded him could produce. And he understood how to maximize each unit.

As our opening drew closer, while somehow still remaining at arms-length, we arranged a small gathering of about twenty people we had come to know along the way. The guest list was a mix of vendors and friends that we had met on the island. Each of them, in their own way, were important to the start of our business. This trial run was an opportunity to not only thank them, but also feature a couple of items we would be serving. If everything went well they would spread the word across the island. Unfortunately, the same could be said if it didn't.

While Sheri mingled with the group and ran the bar, Robert and I were busy in the kitchen cooking. For a starter, he surprised everyone by going off the menu and presenting a Hawaiian dish called laulau. This delicious local plate combines cubes of pork and butterfish, Hawaiian sea salt, and chunks of soft taro wrapped in banana leaves and tied at the top, then steamed. While cooking, the sea salt mingles with the fat of the pork and butterfish to create a flavor and aroma that is impossible to turn down. Those little bundles of tasty goodness, begging to be unwrapped, weren't part of our regular menu, but they made us feel the pride of being able to share a truly Hawaiian experience with our friends.

The night, while anxious, proved a great success and we had made an impression on everyone that turned out. The atmosphere that seemed to be so naturally created, gave us our first glimpse into what it would look like for countless nights to come. There was happy conversation in the air and live music on the stage. Performing was a young, talented singer named David Parsons who, after we opened, would headline every Monday. In a few minutes, he was strumming his guitar, filling the air with island vibes and creating exactly the kind of fun, festive environment that we had envisioned all along.

When we got the word that our permit to open was ready and we could finally start doing business, Sheri and I drove to Lihue within the hour to sign the papers. With so much of the previous month spent waiting on various inspections and government bureaucracies, we didn't waste a minute deciding on the following Monday as our opening date. That gave us only five days to bring in all the product, prep the menu, Hire and train the staff, and cut a radio commercial. I wasn't sure it was enough time, but we couldn't keep sitting on our hands.

From the first day that we walked into that long ignored and forsaken space to survey the spoils of our newfound lease, to the time we finally opened and began realizing our dream, a staggering seven months had passed. While in the end, we were waiting on the county, most of those months were spent with a handful of good people laboring through an enormous amount of work.

Breathtaking Kauai

South shore of Kauai hidden beach

A promise in paradise

We took on a real mess

Foundation to the future

Johnnylove, Sheri, Dave

Adventure to the bamboo

From the grove to the restaurant

Surfboard bar top

Chef Robert

## CHAPTER 13

# Big shoes to fill

W e opened the Garden Island Grille on October 5, 2015. Our former lives, back in Michigan, having been abandoned almost a year to the day. From the moment we arrived, we pursued what was in our hearts. To this point, Sheri and I had already put a tremendous amount of time into the restaurant. It was an outward expression of who we are, and how we wanted to be presented. Every appointment, every detail, was examined, considered, and anguished over with deliberate care and purpose because it was all we knew.

The weekend before was spent taking in deliveries, organizing the walk-in and the dry storage, and setting up the bar and kitchen. Almost every employee we hired was in training. Sheri had the servers buzzing around, trying to impart the importance of every element, while hoping to spot someone setting themselves apart from the rest. Robert and I had the cooks setting up and learning the line, labeling, and stocking product, as well as getting familiar with the cooking equipment. We went over the process of handling each item on the menu from the time it came through the door until it reached the plate.

For most of Sunday, Robert, Sheri, and I prepped everything the menu needed to function. All of our ideas and recipes were coming to life. We cut the chicken and the steaks, roasted the pork, skinned and portioned the fish, butterflied the shrimp, and weighed out the burger. On the six-burner stove, we had sauces simmering, pasta boiling, and red wine reducing. Any pressure I might have otherwise been feeling was quieted for a time as I lost myself in the process, trying not to think about what the next day would bring.

The following morning the three of us were there early. Robert was again flashing that big smile and shaking our shoulders, telling us to relax. The thing was, I couldn't. Our whole life it seemed was on the line. I spent the last thirty years as a tradesman, I had no idea how I would perform in the kitchen, let alone as a restaurant owner. But we pressed on, cooking bacon, reducing a white wine butter sauce, and setting up the line. Building a morning routine, as Robert continuously explained how and why. Sheri, on the other side, was stowing away the bar supplies and setting up the liquor wells, also getting the staff ready for service.

Everything happened in a blur, I don't think Sheri and I spoke to each other all day and when we finally did, there was nothing we wanted but silence. Our minds had been consumed and ultimately overthrown with an experience that to this point, we had yet to encounter ever in our lives. Looking back at the numbers, after a few years had gone by, it wasn't anywhere near as busy as it would eventually be, but at the time it felt like the world had collapsed. I was washed out, drained, and on the verge of crying. The trouble was, if I started, I may never stop, my emotions were that close to the surface. Sheri was the same way. We could barely remember the events of the day, let alone speak about them.

Robert had used up a week of vacation time from his job at the Hyatt to help us get through those first few terrifying days. He knew how important opening day was and the calming effect his presence would bring. We worked long hours together, alternating short breaks throughout the day. When he wasn't busy instructing me, we were both training the rest of the cooks on how we wanted things done. It was exhausting.

Sheri and I would come in early and separate to our own tasks. Robert would show up around nine and scold me for not doing something, or not doing something right. He'd square things up, and we'd cook away another day, sending out plates, restocking the line, heating and re-filling sauces, and turning product. Everything was always fresh. Within a month I was dialing in the ordering process, receiving most items literally on demand.

Sheri spent her day running the bar, making drinks, and trying to get the servers to elevate their game. It was a constant battle. Every night was another meeting involving the serving staff. Sheri would go over, again and again, the absolute need to keep their eyes looking everywhere. It was a speech that Sheri found herself repeating all too often; pay attention to the needs of your customer.

So much of our vision depended on the happy, fun interaction between servers and customers. To get to that point, the servers had to learn the workflow, get into a solid routine, and then strategize on how they could deliver an above-and-beyond experience. I was buried in the kitchen and the prep, making sure we had everything we needed when we needed it, so Sheri was put in the spot to deal with the servers and combat their mistakes and excuses. She spent a lot of her time correcting the same problems with the same people. Challenging all of them to maintain not only the standards we set but to be part of creating the atmosphere that was so important to us.

By some miracle, we had made it through the first week without a mental breakdown. Physically, we were on our feet at least fifteen hours a day, every day. We slept little and ate less. I was so stressed out that my mind felt like it couldn't keep up with the growing demand that was being put on it. This was the craziest ride I had ever been on, at least it had all the stomach flipping, adrenalin spiking earmarks, and it was only just beginning.

Robert had returned to his day job at the Hyatt but continued to work the night shift with us. My mind was more than a little troubled at the thought of not having his reassuring and dogmatic presence around all day, but we had built a comfortable routine together, one that, moving forward, every cook would follow, and I knew I could trust it. By stepping back into his regular day job, he was now placing that mantle squarely on my shoulders.

Knowing my own experience, I still don't know how he did it every day. After his eight-hour shift at the Hyatt, he would bounce through the back door at three like he'd spent the day lounging, and work every night until we closed. I never had a worry when Robert was in the kitchen. He continued in that style for a number of weeks before we could give him a few regular days off. He understood that, and never missed a beat.

It didn't take long to discover that bartenders were hard to find and even harder to trust. We had already experienced enough in that area to back up that conclusion, so Sheri took over full-time. The move put her in front of the customer throughout the day and gave us a face for our restaurant. It also made it easy for her to see both seating areas and head off any possible issues before they arose. She turned out to be a natural, and within a few weeks, she was inventing original house drinks and creating her own infusions. The fresh-squeezed grapefruit and tangerine margaritas as well as the vibrant magenta and sweetly tangy dragon fruit were among our top sellers. Her creativity flowed into every glass.

It's hard to imagine doing this without a partner, and since Sheri and I sought to be a part of our restaurant rather than just own it, we were both lucky to have in each other someone with a high level of passion. Someone whose investment reaches far beyond money. We had begun pouring our hearts into this restaurant long before we ever arrived on Kauai, and the pride of bringing our creation to life and the absolute knowledge of where it could go only intensified that feeling.

In the face of that, we tried to breed those same senses into the serving and bar staff, harshly at times when all other avenues were exhausted. It was draining. Cell phones were a problem. Too many times we found ourselves doing low-grade detective work, discovering that a customer who is waiting for their server has been astonishingly forgotten. Why? In one case, because their server was busy in the parking lot laying in the back seat of their car smoking a cigarette and texting. On the clock. All the while the customer's image of us, of our dream, of everything we worked so hard for, all rests on the service staff doing their job well. It was enough to drive anyone insane.

Meanwhile, Sheri and I were always the first to arrive in the morning and the last to lock up at night, the interim hours completely consumed in the daily activities of running a restaurant. But we loved it, and in the end, that's really what it took. When I wasn't cooking, or needed in the kitchen, I was pouring beers or washing glasses in an attempt to alleviate some of the burdens at the bar, or going table to table, chatting up the guests. She would do the same thing, handling whatever was pressing on her end, then mingling with the crowd, making new friends.

In that way we found ourselves approaching the middle of November and the edge of burnout. Sheri was running the bar and the front of the restaurant while continuing to train and prod the service and host staff. When any block of time, no matter how small, would present itself, she used it to create and blend the infusions used in all the cocktails throughout the day. All of the mixes that went into our drinks at the bar were either freshly squeezed or made by hand. From the simple syrup to the fresh fruit juices, the sweet and sour, and a killer bloody mary, Sheri had devised them all and continuously kept a rotating stock.

The demands were endless and there was always something to do. Twice a week I was running to Costco between shifts for the few things we needed there. Every four days I was in early, draining and re-filling the fryers, and every Sunday I thought I'd save a few bucks and show up at dawn to clean the vent hood. All that was sprinkled around the enormous amount of time I spent in the kitchen and working the line. I was worried I'd have too much free time, so I also coordinated the live music we had every night.

We looked at Thanksgiving as a chance for a day off and we grabbed it. The loss of a day's income was the furthest thing from our minds. We were closing for the holiday. It would be our first day off in six weeks. The importance of family time for our staff was an easy and acceptable excuse, but the truth was, I don't think either one of us could go another day without a break. It wasn't that we were so hands-on that we couldn't let go, there simply wasn't anybody to let it go to. At this point, no one on our staff had stood out with the flags of possible management, and we trusted no one with the reputation of our restaurant, even for half a day. As modestly as I can say it, the restaurant simply couldn't run without us, at least not the way we wanted it to.

Once we hit December, I started noticing that my insides weren't kicking my ass quite so much and I could breathe marginally better. The constant pressure was ebbing away and with it came a renewed energy. The restaurant was coming together and our talks were more about what's next than just mere survival. A curtain was parting and we were understanding the restaurant business. We found the day-to-day operations from open to close to be straightforward. It was filling the key roles with the right people that was proving difficult.

Labor continued its up-and-down trend as we entered the new year. On an island this small the pool is limited to begin with, so when the hotels and resorts, with their bottomless health plans and escalating salaries, take the top two-thirds, what's left is anyone's guess. The addition and subtraction of the staff, whether it was their decision or ours, was an ongoing theme and I've learned over the years that it doesn't get any better. Outside of a handful of two, or three in each area, the rest of the staff was constantly in flux, but we had a heart that was beating, a trust that was forming, and a family we were building. Everything was pointing in the right direction.

Before his shift began one afternoon, early in the new year, Robert came to us privately, head down, and told us he could no longer work with us. He said it was nothing that we did, or failed to do, but that it was personal, and he was sorry. We had heard through the often-unreliable coconut wireless, that he had taken a leave of absence from the Hyatt which had begun sometime in

December. He was somber and not very forthcoming, a reserved, private, and proud Hawaiian. We were, of course, shocked.

Before Christmas, Robert was hit hard by a sudden death in his family, a young man he was very close to. We did everything we could for him, but his mood continued to drift downward. Although the death of someone close is a tremendous weight to bear, he seemed to be carrying more than that. He kept his emotions to himself, and nobody got in. Robert always felt like a brother to me, and he had Sheri's unwavering love and respect, so it was difficult to watch him shut down. He began saying less and less and distancing himself more and more. It was heartbreaking.

Very few people in my life have made the kind of impact that Robert did. From the moment he walked into our lives, with his big smile and even bigger heart, he made us feel a part of this island. I knew before I ever discovered what he did for a living, that he was someone I wanted to know. He demanded and expected so much from himself when it came to quality and integrity, that he shed that light on the people around him.

He had brought that same light to an area of the restaurant that needed it most. His tireless work in the kitchen with me will always be a memory I treasure. It was the most intense time of my life. But he was more than that. He made us laugh, and he came to work with a vigor that was infectious. He threw out pidgin words like choke and dakine and made us puzzle over them until we guessed their meaning. He never verbally boasted about his heritage, he just stood tall with an ease and confidence that was all Robert and showed you what it meant to be Hawaiian.

In the early months, we would sit at one of the bar tables after the rest of the crew had left and just talk, often to our own detriment, till one in the morning. We would always start with the restaurant, but the conversation soon drifted between our stories of Michigan and Robert's stories of Kauai. He loved our tales and traditions of a life lived amidst the backdrop of the Great Lakes, but his eyes would sparkle and the laughter would come easy as he spoke of a smaller world, and an earlier life on Niihau, catching lobsters with his father and learning to throw the net.

He brought us into his life and showed us his culture. He shared Hawaiian legends, and told us island history the way he learned it, passed down from generations. He told us again how far back his family name went, and the weight that it carried. But he also enlightened us about his mischievous teenage years, when he would take the trail down to Pakala Beach because the surf was up and the waves were full of riders, and he would trade in his slippers for a better pair off the pile. Robert, like a handful of other people we've met, brought us something unexpected.

In the pursuit of what we had envisioned for the restaurant, the kitchen, surprisingly, was the area we were the proudest of. The one that came the closest to hitting the mark every day. With so much of it that I didn't understand in the beginning, all the mysteries of a world I had no experience in, possibly no business in, I still shake my head, baffled at how it came to be that way.

Regardless of how good the food is, if the process to prepare and plate it is thoughtless and confusing, then the result is going to reflect that. The goal is to make as few tweaks or changes as possible along the way, to recipes, plating, and prep, to provide a more consistent experience for the guests. Robert was able to address that right from the beginning and worked with each cook on every step required to create a beautiful plate. Which brought us out as a contender on the island from the first day, and we accomplished this from a cooking space no bigger than an average walk-in closet.

With the equipment in place, our kitchen is no more than a small hallway. Fryers, grills, and a six-burner stove line one side, with the vent hood roaring above. The other side is taken up with two reach-in coolers topped by a long, white cutting board. Lining the available walls are an array of shelves neatly stacked with plates, bowls, baskets, sauté pans, seasonings, and anything else that is quickly needed. A pair of cooks in blue chef coats, doing completely different things, work in tandem to finish every part of the plate at the same time.

Inside that little spot it's like a Trojan horse. Drawers, doors, and lids open up, and a hundred items come popping out. Everything has miraculously found a place. Every product needed to cook and plate the menu is right there at their fingertips. Our everyday prep guy was the heart of that department, but each cook was responsible for the prepping, cleaning, and filling of their own station, as well as making sure there was a backup of every item in the walk-in.

We've had a lot of people tell us that the kitchen was too small, that it couldn't support the restaurant, that we should block off one of the dining rooms, maybe sell t-shirts and shot glasses out of there. No imagination, no will to succeed.

During our summer of construction, a consultant from one of the big culinary institutes in New York ambled through the front doors looking for the bathroom. He looked around and seemed to take a keen interest in our kitchen. Once he discovered that we were the owners, he proceeded to explain all the reasons that a space of that size will never work. I guess while on vacation, he wasn't able to leave the job behind. He told us in no uncertain terms that we could never do the volume out of the kitchen that was required to sustain the restaurant. Through it all, he offered no positive advice and ended his monologue of doom by saying we would be out of business within a year. That was his assessment based on the industry odds. But we had the passion within us to take what we had and make it work.

Knowing our size limitations, it required us to create a system between each cook that would allow them to work quickly and efficiently while using the least amount of space. It all came together, even in the harshest opinion of professionals, and proved its worth by pumping out over five-hundred plates a day when the tourist season hits its peak, all with almost no customer complaints.

As we worked side-by-side, Robert continuously walked me through every process of the kitchen set-up, break-down, and cleaning. We implemented procedures for opening, shift change, and closing for every cook to follow, and outlined which non-cooking duties each side of the two-man line would be charged with. We went over not just every product, but the vessels they would be cooked, stored, and served in. We made sure there was enough ease of access for each cook to reach the items that would likely be used the most.

When we had worked our way through the menu and had everything arranged so a two-man line could run efficiently, we were left with six items that required a steam table. Since we started this course in kitchen configuring, we had been challenged at every turn, these last few key elements were not going to deter us. The only available space remaining in the entire kitchen was a twelve-inch-wide stainless-steel cabinet between the fryers and the six-burner stove.

We never ordered a steam table because frankly, I didn't even know what one was, or how to use it for that matter. But for some reason, we did order a three-crock soup warmer. That's what I said to Robert, and he looked at me like I had two heads. I was making a joke, I thought it was kind of funny, one has absolutely nothing to do with the other. He didn't seem like he got the joke, however, because he asked me where it was.

Turns out the soup warmer was its own steam table. Who knew? The basin held electrically heated water to keep the soup hot, only we weren't serving any soup on the menu. The entire apparatus fit the narrow space we had like it was made to be there. My stainless guy re-designed the top to fit the six containers we needed. With everything in place, the kitchen was done.

Entwined throughout the many days we spent organizing and establishing the rhythm of the kitchen, we listened as Robert hammered home the idea that when a plate is set in front of you, your eyes are the first thing to devour it. The three of us spent many afternoons discussing how every item on the menu would be presented, and how certain sauces and reductions would be used to add color, flavor, and pizzazz to the plate. When we were done, we had a visual of what every plate should look like when it leaves the kitchen.

Over the years our cooks have taken this imaginative practice to another level. Plate vision they call it, and everything that goes out to a table is a work of art because they're constantly competing with each other. The cooks are on display through a large window that looks out over the front dining room. The view they have affords them the unique opportunity to watch the experience unfold as the plate arrives at the table and the camera comes out long before the silverware. It's a moment of pride in that kitchen when a customer acknowledges the cooks with a thumbs-up, or a high five across the room because they weren't expecting a five-star exhibition.

That was Robert, challenging every cook and instilling a sense of pride in the people that worked around him. It was his knowledge, patience, and persistence that prepared us for the multitude of untold pitfalls we would encounter and the solutions they required. His sudden departure left a huge hole, not just in Sheri and me, but in the entire restaurant. He would not say what was fueling this decision to abandon both of his jobs, only that he had to take care of a few things. I knew enough not to push him, but we were worried.

It was impossible to imagine our restaurant without Robert. Those first couple of months, until we got our legs under us, were flat-out hell. It was all at once the world's longest cram session. A continuous effort to keep from breaking. At times it felt like an all-out race to not look like a fool, but Robert was always there, and sometimes just his presence was enough.

We tried to bring him in as a partner, but he wasn't interested. We tried to make him at least a General Manager, anything to show him how much he meant to us, but he refused them all. At the time we didn't understand why this change had come over him, and it was heartbreaking. No amount of asking, or show of concern could draw out the reason.

Robert's personal life was private, and outside of his family, his real family, he kept it that way. If he had sent signals to either one of us, we had missed them. We couldn't avoid the sadness in our hearts brought on by his increasing silence. He worked his final shift, regretfully said goodbye to Sheri and I, briefly gazed around the restaurant, and quietly slipped through the back door. We wouldn't know till much later about his private struggle, one he chose to keep secret, but his impact on our lives and his influence on the restaurant will always remain.

## CHAPTER 14

# Roberts gift

O ur food was incredible and the presentation belayed any thoughts that you were in a typical bar and grill. Our dream of an old-school Hawaiian-style restaurant in the heart of old Koloa Town had taken shape, and we were becoming a popular place. We keep a steady pace throughout the year, with a couple of slow-er-than-average months in the spring and fall, but the two weeks that follow Christmas are nothing like the rest. For that festive and merry season, tropical holiday seekers from all over the world descend on our small island. The hotels, resorts, and vacation rentals are filled to capacity, the roads are jammed with rental cars, and the number of people clamoring to get into our restaurant more than doubles.

In Koloa, all the small-town charm, holiday excitement, and Christmas spirit you could ever envision is dressed-up and on display for the occasion. If a reminder is needed that the holiday is alive and well in paradise, then a twelve-foot Santa, dressed in Hawaiian wear and flip-flops usually does the trick. Gripping a towering surfboard in his pudgy right hand while the left is busy locked in an animated pinky-thumb wave known as the shaka, this reimagined holiday icon welcomes everyone.

The festival of lights and merriment continues into the restaurant, and by the time the stage heats up with the sounds of the season, the entire place has reached a mad rush. The wait staff is running, Sheri at the bar is in full swing, and the boys and I are slammed in the kitchen. It's an overwhelming, high-pressure, high-stakes situation when the four-foot ticket rail that the cooks are looking at is jammed full of orders, and the machine won't stop spitting them out.

The two guys working together in tandem are constantly in motion, continuously cooking, plating, filling, and prepping just to keep up. The part of the night that felt like you were being pulled tighter than a piano wire only consumed about two hours, but the intensity of that time drained every internal resource that could be tapped. After the last order is sent out the window, as beautifully plated as the first, and before the clean-up begins, the cooks slip out for a smoke. Their frayed nerves soaking in a few minutes of silence the back parking lot offers.

Through it all the kitchen has only gotten better, and the pride that flows out of that sweltering arena is felt not just by Sheri and I but on every plate that goes to a table. That was Robert's gift to us, a legacy that he would be proud of. He left his mark on the restaurant in so many ways that it was difficult to imagine that he was no longer a part of it. He was the pillar of strength that supported us from the beginning. The absence of his confidence, the rock we leaned on so often, was another hurdle laid out before us that we would have to get past. His belief in himself was contagious and infected me with enough poise and certainty to continue the lessons that he had put into practice.

We had already lost Johnnylove. Once the restaurant opened and there was nothing left to build, he decided to go into landscaping and spend his days outside. We've stayed in touch as much as we can. I do miss his rants though, and his passion for the Hawaiian sovereignty to reclaim their land. At times we had no idea what he was saying. When he got rolling his mix of English, pidgin, and beer became another language altogether. But he was always passionate about his beliefs and we loved him for it. Now, Robert had moved on as well, leaving a gaping hole not only in the hearts of the staff, but in the soul of the restaurant.

As time unwound itself, and the months continued to spool out, until we had quite a pile of them, Sheri and I were still logging enormous hours. In the kitchen, I was always just one guy away, and the front of the house was at times a revolving door. We did, however, have a handful of people that displayed heart and desire, a really good core that we could build around.

Over the next two years, we went along in that way, growing the inner circle of employees we could trust, the ones who gave themselves back to the restaurant. And working with a few on how to take that next step. We were finally moving to a place where co-workers were challenging each other, instead of just Sheri and I making all the demands. There still appeared to be nobody waiting just over the horizon, or a member of our staff a little closer, that we were willing to give up even partial management to, and pay them accordingly.

As the Garden Island Grille slid into its third year, we were pretty happy with where we were, there was more to be done certainly, but even through our exhaustion, we were proud of what we had turned our lives into. Sheri and I had somehow, through our sheer determination, left stable and comfortable careers to dive head first into a dream that we knew nothing about, and against all odds we were succeeding. We were getting to the bottom of not just the ins and outs of the restaurant business, but the ups and down's as well. If in the beginning, we thought it was more than we had bargained for, we now at least knew a simple truth. That it would always be that way.

We would often stand at the railing near the courtyard in front of the stage after everyone had left, and just look out over the restaurant. It was the only time we would allow ourselves to fully let our guard down and just relax in the quiet surroundings. We still could not believe we were where we were, living a life that at one time only resided in our heads. We were two people who did something that even our closest friends secretly thought we couldn't. We were taking a road that to them was unconventional, bordering on reckless, and they couldn't understand why.

By this time, we had been written up in the island news a couple of times, and according to Trip Advisor, out of three hundred and fifty places you could eat on the island, we were listed in the top fifteen. On the south shore alone, we had been as high as number three. Our concept had turned into a restaurant generating well over a million dollars in sales annually and we were consistently ranked by guests as one of the best on the island. So, we were doing something right. We had figured a daily break-even number, and within the first week we were operating in the black, and by the end of the first year, we had recovered all of our start-up debt. The number of restaurants that fail in the first two years of operation is staggering, we had made it well beyond that, and our reputation was growing.

Early in our third-year news came to us that chef Robert had passed away. It hit me like a sledgehammer. Robert never explained why he left us, and it hurt that we didn't understand at the time what led him to make that decision. Or that we never had the chance to say goodbye. We learned that he had undergone his own battle with a disease that was aggressive and intent on winning, and in the end, had accomplished its goal. We had lost a true friend. One that for his own reasons had drifted away to find peace in whatever ways he could, but he will always be a part of our lives.

Robert is someone I will never forget. How could I? He came into our lives when we needed him most, and he touched us in ways that will forever change us. The memories of him shatter my thoughts in the quiet moments. It could be a song on our mix, or a morning when I'm there early, opening up, and he'll be there watching from the doorway, shaking his head and smiling that smile.

I had an extra chef coat of his, two actually, still in the package. Kanahele, his surname, emblazoned appropriately over the heart. We displayed one of them during the week of his funeral, with a note explaining everything he meant to us. It's something I still hold onto as my own totem of Robert's memory. The other we gave to his family, as they dined in our restaurant shortly after he was buried. For such a great chef who never left the island, ours was the last coat he ever wore.

His death, because he was so young, brought us to the realization that life is fleeting, and while we were putting in one-hundred-hour weeks for two and a half years, that same life was clicking by twice as fast. For that period, our existence was centered around the restaurant. We got home each night around eleven o'clock, made a snack, and went to bed. Only to wake up early and convince our tired feet to hit the floor and do it all over again. We met a lot of people, and we made several friends, but those relationships were kept alive by their appearance at the bar or sitting at a table.

The restaurant owned us, and we knew that. It took away any ability to have a life outside of it. We were chained to the evil step-mother and bore all the weight that comes with it. We were forced to regretfully decline one invitation after another, by people who wanted to know us better, but there was nothing we could do.

Going through that period of endless work and constant movement, the endless hours between waking and sleeping, took away something physically from us. And at our age, it's taken a long time to get it back, if we ever will. We were both running out of energy, and with no end in sight, something had to change. We needed to make a change.

A quick look at the numbers told us what we already knew. Wednesday was going to become a day to look forward to. Struggling to reach the break-even mark on too many of those nights made this an easy decision. So, with no other alternatives in sight, and knowing from experience that we couldn't be away from the place for more than two or three hours before a problem arose, we closed the restaurant one day a week. It may sound crazy, but for us, it was the smartest thing we ever did. What made the whole thing prophetic was that the musician who played on Wednesday night came to me, hat in hand the week before, and said he was moving to the mainland, and that night would be his last. I never had to break the news to him.

## CHAPTER 15

# Building the family

W hen we left the Great Lakes, with its multiple seasons and varied climates, and sought a life among the people of the tropics, we brought with us an inherent will to work hard. It took me a while to figure it out, but by my mid-twenties I was pretty well coming around. It's been labeled over the decades as a Midwestern work ethic, slapped onto an area of the country that has survived through generations of farming and ranching, from dawn till dusk. The Heartland of America. A collection of states whose people are never afraid to plunge their hands into the fertile soil of the American dream.

Over the past thirty years, I had worked hard for what I had, as did Sheri. We spent most of our lives around people for whom a hard day's work was part of their lifestyle. With that in mind, I figured finding good employees and setting up a pretty solid work-force would be the least of our concerns. But living on an island was different. The issue continually forced its way to the top of our list of challenges from the day we opened. We had never factored in or even considered, the laid-back tropical lifestyle that so naturally pervades the island and seems to infect most of the labor pool we were drawing from. Once the high-paying resorts have had their fill, we were left to feed on the remainder. Not unlike fishing, we have to throw a lot of them back because they don't meet the minimum requirements. A few have resurfaced after growing in someone else's pond.

Nothing happens fast on this island. There's too much good surf, sun, and fun for it to be any other way. For the vacationer who finally blocked off a couple of weeks to escape the demands of a hectic life, that feeling is what you went searching for. The whole reason we're drawn to the tropics is to seek all that sunshine and white sand, and for a moment, just unplug and slow down. So many of the people who move to the islands are seeking out that same slow pace.

On the few occasions that Sheri and I spent vacationing on these islands, I found that easygoing, hang-loose atmosphere, quite appealing. Now, as someone desperately in need of some of those same people to help grow our business, it was frustrating. Finding anyone to do more than what the minimum required was like searching through the grassy knoll, seeking something that can't be found. There were so few exceptions to this rule, that we zealously clung to the ones we were determined to hold on to. But for every diamond we found, there was twice as much rough to search through.

Tony could never figure out the POS system. Every mistake, and there was a lot, he would blame on the computer. It was always the computer's fault. Credit cards ran on the wrong bill, food rung up on the wrong ticket, too many beers, too many wines, the list went on and on, and always the computer. He would argue with Sheri vehemently over what he knew was not his fault, even in the face of mounting evidence to the contrary. After two weeks, and that was generous, we were over it, and let him go. He was the guy you couldn't teach anything to, and we went through more than our share of training sessions because he already knew it all.

I was in the kitchen one day after a busy lunch, cleaning and re-filling my side of the line while my partner did his when our hostess that day hands me a torn piece of scrap paper across the polished granite of the pass-thru window. Before I could even look at it, she calls out that it was her two-week notice, the job is too hard. So, with the mystery gone, I didn't bother to read it and handed it back to her. She had been there for two days, and honestly, I'm not sure I even knew her name. That's not normally my practice, but with Sheri hiring her side, it does happen.

"Don't you need that for my files or something?" She said.

I could not imagine why we would possibly have files on this girl, and if we did, what would be in them? I suppose maybe just the torn piece of scrap paper that was now fluttering between her fingers. I told her there was no need for a notice, she could quit now, and I was horrified to hear my father's own words out of my mouth, but that's how I felt. I guess he did too. I had long ago discovered that once an employee has given notice, keeping them around for two weeks was an incredible waste of time and money, especially for a position so easily filled.

While she stood there lingering, I went back to what I was doing undeterred and told her there was nothing left to say. But she continued sniping at me through the window, telling me that I owed her two weeks, and going on about the notice, and a lawyer, and when she started raising her voice, I drew her into the back room.

I said look, I can't believe I have to explain this to you. You offered me the privilege of your service for the next two weeks and

I have elected to waive that privilege. She stormed out the door yelling to everyone, including our guests, how I was ripping her off.

I hired a dishwasher to fill a couple of nights, a young guy that had shown up a few times looking for a job. Anything sir, he would say. He always brought his family; his wife and small baby, like they were needed to secure a position. Every time he would come in to see me his manners were impeccable, if not a bit over the top. His need to make sure I knew how hard he worked dominated the discussion as if he alone possessed this skill.

I set him up with the weekend night shift in the dish room. The first weekend was like a dream, the kid caught on fast, seemed ambitious, and did a great job. It was looking like the dishwashers as a group were becoming the most dependable part of the restaurant. We needed to figure out how to bring that over to the rest of the crew. I was dropping whatever else I was doing and covering for a cook, or jumping in to serve tables, almost every day. Rarely did Sheri, or I, ever fill in for a dishwasher. We did, but not often.

When the kid shows up the next weekend, he doesn't seem quite the same, there's something off. I make sure he still understands what to do, and how much soap and sanitizer to use. He looked pretty focused because he was staring intently into the second sink like there was a fortune to be read down there. I regained his attention, got him going, and went back to the front of the house.

It was Saturday night, busy, as the weekends always are. Kalani was on the Aloha Stage, holding everyone's attention as he sang about the islands, his songs lamenting the passing of a time that will never return. The servers and food runners were bustling table to table, and the cooks, in their special language, were banging out one order after another. It was in the middle of this orchestrated chaos that Sheri pulled me aside and told me to take a peek in the dish room. When I did, I found our dishwasher doing kung-fu moves and spin kicking the air, like a bad version of Bruce Lee. I thought I'd seen it all, but nope, not even close. I asked him what the hell was wrong with him, and told him to get back to work. Put some of that energy into the dishes.

Later in the night when the clean-up was underway, I could hear Sheri, her voice raised, back in the area where we kept the karate kid. She was asking him, as I had earlier, what the hell was going on, and why everything was piling up. He didn't seem to know. He looked lost, like all this stuff suddenly appeared, and he was confused. I'm sure it was drugs, it had to be. Three of us pitched in to help finish his job that night.

I was making decisions on what to do with this kid, so I spoke to him after work that night. I told him what was on my mind concerning the drugs, and how we weren't here to babysit. We discussed in detail, that when you come to work, that's what you do, you work, it's not playland. He stared back at me with vacant eyes, nodding his head in agreement. Nothing like the kid who, just a few weeks prior, stood before me with his small family in tow, pleading for a job.

I said I'd see him tomorrow night and sent him out the door. I still wasn't sure if anything I said even got through to him. My dilemma was solved the next night when we caught him smoking meth behind the dumpsters while taking out the garbage. My suspicions were heightened from the night before, so I was keeping a close eye on him. Strange way of taking care of the family.

When we first opened, we hired a prep chef that impressed us on paper with his ten years of experience, and his self-proclaimed, 'mad knife skills.' I've always tried to find the best in people, but he couldn't seem to figure out the job. With all his alleged experience, he struggled to understand and correlate the prep to fit the menu. Robert was doing most of the work while trying to train the guy, and complaining to me every night that he wasn't getting it.

After finding him in the walk-in time and time again, staring around, seemingly baffled by all the product in there, we knew we were going to need to upgrade that position. Prep, after all, was the most important part of the menu. Nothing that we saw showed us any indication of the type of experience he had advertised. Robert spoke his mind at any cost and started calling him the paper chef, to his face, trying to challenge him to reach higher. He did look good on paper.

I had to pull Robert aside and tell him to maybe ease up on the guy, let's see what he's got before you run him off too soon. He had a way of looking at me sometimes that spoke louder than his words. That was the look I was getting.

"For real! Come on boss, it's been two weeks, I've seen what he's got already. No need." He was always so direct, even if the subject was standing right next to him, which in this case he was.

I guess that was the last straw. Rather than rise to the challenge and prove him wrong, the guy threw down his apron, gathered up his knives, of which he only ever used one, and stormed out the door yelling that he quit. Robert, being Robert, just laughed and said, 'good, let him run away, mo bettah we hire my friend Romy'.

I stood there a little pissed off that Robert would put me in this position with no prep guy, I was already stretched as thin as I could get. Then it quickly dawned on me that Robert and I were doing ninety percent of it anyway, I was paying a guy to do a job he clearly couldn't do. In his own way, right or wrong, Robert was forcing me to see that.

Somewhere in his words and actions, he was telling me that I needed to fix this, that someone doing ten percent of their job wasn't going to cut it. Even with his aggressive approach, I knew he was right. With the kitchen so dependent on prep, I had to find someone who could actually keep up with the demand. I also knew that among all the applications sitting on my kitchen counter at home, not one of them contained that person. All this went through my mind in the few seconds we stood there, and then I remembered something.

"Wait, who's Romy?"

Romeo came to us as a surprise, and along with Robert, they personified our relationship with the island. We took from it many things to provide for our restaurant and counted on local growers for so many items on our product list. Everything from fruits and vegetables, to beef, fresh herbs, and sea salt, we acquired from vendors through the bounty of the island. But, we also gave back as much as we could in so many small ways. One of those contributions sits at the heart of our small town.

Placed within a large circle of concrete and grass stands a monument dedicated to the many years and generations of migrant workers who came to Kauai to labor in the sugar cane fields. Throughout the 1800s, men and women from China, Portugal, Japan, and the Philippines, fled their homeland and rolled the dice on a more prosperous future in that once-booming industry. Their families, through many generations, have since stayed and lived their lives here. The monument tells their story and plots their history. Weathered and in need of restoration, it nonetheless portrays a significant time in the great past of this foremost island. Our little town of Koloa had been the site of the first sugar plantation in all of Hawaii.

In early October, just days before the restaurant opened, Sheri read a clipping from our local newspaper that said a fundraiser for that exact project was underway. It was perfect. We were quietly looking for a way to give something back to a community that welcomed us, that took us in as the immigrants that we were, and with our love of history, it was the right fit.

After e-mailing a couple of times to find out more about the project, we donated the full amount of their goal anonymously. Over time the monument was restored and we were comfortable knowing that we were a large part of it, even if no one else did. The island, however, must have taken notice and marked it, as I have now gone over to the side of believing these things, because Romeo was everything you could ever want in an employee, running the entire prep show and doing the work of three guys sometimes.

It turned out he worked with Robert at the Hyatt, had been there for twenty-five years, and wanted a second job that would fit around his schedule. He was putting his daughter through college and needed a little extra. I hired him the next day. After a quick tour of the dry storage and the walk-in, I gave him a menu and the top-secret folder with all the recipes. He and Robert started in on it while I set up the line. Romeo turned out to be a dream. Rarely do you find an employee, who in just a few minutes time, can look around the walk-in cooler, and know exactly what his priorities are. His instincts were so sharp that he routinely knew what the cooks needed before they did.

For us to have the kind of place we wanted, the type of place we had thought about for years, it was going to take quite a strong group of people that could reach the standard that Sheri and I were setting, and by being in the trenches and working all day, every day, that bar was pretty high. As far back as the first day, we were pushing and challenging all of our people, making it clear from the beginning that as long as they were willing to work hard and really wanted it, they could climb as high as they wanted to in this restaurant.

The constant burden of hiring and firing, people quitting, and the endless training was taxing. We had a solid core of people that seemed to care about our restaurant and their place in it. They had heart and we recognized it. That group wasn't always perfect, but they had gone beyond our expectations at times and had ultimately gained our trust. The problems and the turnover came from a handful of employees that simply didn't care. They were there to pick up a paycheck and the heart played no role in how they treated the restaurant or the job they chose.

Sheri was running the bar full-time because the two guys we had originally hired for that position were both stealing inside the first week, while we were there. As if we were too stupid to know the difference. They both gained a new perspective. For that reason, I have cameras everywhere. Some of them are disguised so they can't be seen, and while I don't sit in an office staring at the monitors all day, or ever, when something seems hokey that's the first place I go.

For all the trouble we had with so many employees, from hoping they'll show up, to equally hoping they don't melt down when they do, we had an amazing core of people that got it, that understood what it meant to reach higher and become more, and they made me want to come back day after day. We had to go through so many just to find the few we could trust to uphold the standards we had set. And if we thought we could ever have time away from the restaurant, we needed people we could trust.

One of those, and probably the one I would put first in line is Jeric, my lead cook. He's made himself so valuable to us that over the past two years we have raised his hourly wage so that he's one of the highest-paid non-hotel chefs on the island. The law doesn't allow someone in his position to receive a share of any tip money, otherwise, he would have earned that as well. He's exactly the kind of person I wish I had ten of, and he came that way, unadvertised and unvarnished.

We plucked him from the Italian place next door where he worked the sauté line. Out behind the restaurant, where I spent time when I had to get away, I would see him and chat him up a couple of times a week. I always came away shaking my head, wondering why I hadn't hired this kid yet. We had a more or less unspoken pact with the owners of the other shops and restaurants that made up Koloa Town, that we wouldn't steal each other's employees. It was tough at times, my friend Marn owned the ice cream shop up the boardwalk and I desperately wanted his manager. Jeric was in that category. I stuck to the unwritten rules and brought it up only to Sheri.

We were in such desperate need that she was of the mind to just offer him more money than what he was making, but I wasn't ready to piss off the neighbors just yet. She said fine, see if he wants to pick up a couple of shifts and see what happens. I hadn't thought about that, just a few hours a week and he can come to his own conclusions. I never brought up the topic before, because he seemed pretty settled in and full-time where he was. I didn't like the idea of outright soliciting and stealing a good employee from another restaurant, especially the one directly beside us.

Out of the blue, he asked me if I had any nights available, the pizza place had been, little by little, cutting his hours. I was surprised at his request, as I was about to ask him the same thing. By necessity, my schedule had me on the line working the grill six nights a week, so the options were many. He picked the two that worked for him, and by the end of the second night, he had not only perfected the job, but he had also won over the entire staff. To no surprise, he put in his notice next door and came over full-time.

Still looking up at thirty, he carries himself with a confidence that for once isn't arrogance covering up inability, but more of a belief that he can do anything that you put in front of him, and he does. He's got such a heart and love for the restaurant that it shows in every detail, from the time he clocks in until the final mopping.

For all the energy expelled, and focus consumed while on the clock, it doesn't stop there. Drinks after work, where the staff unwinds after the day, known as pau hana, brings out his macabre sense of humor. With his relentless impersonations of co-workers and customers, mixed in with stories of growing up in the Philippines, planting rice, and chasing snakes, he's one of the funniest people I've ever met. In a sea of senseless employees, we managed to attract and keep a few really good ones, and when we watch that group in action, it makes us proud to own the restaurant.

By working the restaurant day and night, year after year, we learned the business from the inside out. By grasping the tenor and vibe from day to day, we were able to build the kind of atmosphere we wanted, and the kind of work environment we expected, and as a result, our group became tighter, and we learned to count on each other a little more.

Through just the first three years we had served hundreds of thousands of guests, went through a lot of changes, and put our minds and our bodies through hell. At the same time, we turned absolutely no restaurant experience into a business that was continuing to gain momentum, and our reviews were showing it. We had climbed to within the top five percent of all restaurants on the island and digging our heels in, it's where we've stayed. Think about that. We are in a highly competitive industry on an island where restaurants compete to attract a set number of people. Yet, even with the advantages the big resorts have, with their world-renowned chefs in tall poofy hats, our customers were still giving us higher marks and pushing us farther up the charts. Sheri and I were proud of what we had accomplished so far, but there was still so much more to do.

We tossed an idea across an ocean and chased it to Kauai, and under more duress, and way more work than I ever imagined, we turned that idea into reality. We had completely steered our life in another direction, and by our determination and sacrifice, we were finding success. The life we led up to this point may have prepared us for the work that was necessary, but our steadfast drive, and outright resolution to walk among giants, is what pushed us through.

The vision we set out to reach, the image that had been building in our minds almost from the day we met, has been difficult to obtain. The passion and commitment that Sheri and I have put into the restaurant long before we ever opened, has never waned. Even with all the day-to-day frustrations and the continuous problems we had in the labor department, we still had so many nights that were pure magic.

It was the entertainment coming from the stage that always seemed to bring everyone together. A simple dinner reservation, expecting nothing more than a night out, will likely find you in the courtyard learning the hula, or singing the back-up to Sweet

Caroline, or if you're lucky, dancing with our dishwasher, but it will be a night you'll never forget.

## CHAPTER 16

# The heart of our dream

As far back as our earliest days together, Sheri and I were always of the same mind when we spoke of atmosphere and the feeling we wanted our customers to experience if we ever owned a restaurant, whether it be in tropical Hawaii, or Saugatuck, Michigan. Many cold winter nights were spent in our garage, with a portable campfire at the open door, and a small furnace raging inside, while our usual band of friends loitered in and out, with drinks in their hands.

Conversation would tend to happen in groups, with certain members of each flowing into others. A topic being debated by a few might spread throughout the rest until everyone is suddenly interested in why Kelli should, or shouldn't buy a new boat in the spring. Then Brenda would call everyone together with a bottle of tequila in the air, and we'd all line up in front of a shot glass.

That simple ease in which everybody interacted with each other and felt comfortable doing it was exactly the atmosphere we wanted to duplicate in our restaurant. We didn't just want customers, we wanted friends and we had no idea how to do that with guests that were continuously coming and going, except to be there all the time, to be the constant. So, we were. Day and night we worked to create a climate of togetherness, of family, of being a part of something more than the plate in front of you.

Sheri, at the bar, has brought so many people together who would never have met otherwise, just by introducing everyone sitting there to each other. She would get the conversation started and then back away to do other things. Meanwhile, a vacation friendship began to burn. We often find them back again, all together, after a zipline trip, or canyon hike, seeking a larger table.

I was wandering around the restaurant on a Thursday night, shaking hands and making sure everyone was happy when I stopped to chat with a nice couple seated at a table for two. The wife grabbed my arm after I introduced myself and thanked me for a wonderful night. I asked them where they were visiting from, as most of our guests are vacationing from somewhere. She said northern California, and I said really, what town? He said Crescent City, and I mentioned that we'd been there, in fact, we had lunch at the Chart Room while passing through on our way to Oakland for our final move.

The wife was surprised, but even more so was the couple at the next table over, who exclaimed they were also from Crescent City, out by Lake Earl. Well, one thing led to another, and they got to talking and sharing stories. I offered a hand as they began sliding their tables together before I quietly excused myself. I wasn't surprised to still find them laughing and talking nearly two hours later.

The following year they were back, both couples. This time they were traveling together, asking if I remembered them. I meet thousands of people a year, but when they brought up Crescent City, I recalled instantly our shared memory and the table that joined in.

They said they met at our place and they haven't separated since. They came in, of course, for dinner, but also to thank us for bringing together a friendship that was under their noses the whole time.

There was a line in the first radio ad I ever did that said, 'enjoy a great night with friends you bring, or friends you meet', and it happened to us more times than I can count. Winding through the tables and around the bar, a spirit of togetherness and family would get two strangers talking, usually men going on about their team, and before you know it the tables are pushed together and the women would join in the conversation.

Couples and families from all over the world have met and discovered new relationships at our restaurant, finding something unexpected on their vacation. It's a feeling I can't describe, noticing two couples you brought together at the bar the night before, occupying a table the next night. They would be laughing and chatting like old friends, giving no indication that they had just met.

On and on it's gone like that, the same people coming back every year, dropping in as soon as they land, to make sure we were still there and grabbing some take-out for their first night. Everyone asks if we remember them. I try to, but I can't. There are just too many people in between, too many faces to put a name to. If they come in enough during their stay on the island, which many of them do, I have a better shot the following year, but a single conversation that was memorable to someone may not stick with me a year or two later.

An experience I'm not likely to forget, however, and the one that is always foremost in my mind, took place at a table during a quiet happy hour. With only a scattering of guests, I decided to leave the line to my cooking partner and say hello to the few people that were there. As I approach the last table, which was currently held by a well-dressed older couple, I can see that they have *The Ultimate Kauai Guidebook* sitting in front of them.

If you own a business here in Hawaii that caters to tourism, or at least, in some way depends on it, then you need to be in *The Ultimate Guidebook*. There's one for every island. They review everything from hiking trails, helicopter rides, and tourist adventures, all the way to hotels, resorts, and the multitude of restaurants, food trucks, take-out windows, and lunch counters that dot the islands. Their writers sneak in unannounced and unknown, scrutinizing every part of their visit without ever giving away their hand. That is until the new edition comes out, and every tourist visiting the island judges you by those sacred words. Holding nothing back, their editors allow the full truth to be exposed, and good or bad, it's in there. That guidebook carries a tremendous amount of weight, and to be in it, with a good review, means everything.

In the native language of the Hawaiian people, 'ono' is the word that is used to express how delicious, or impressive something is. It's the term *The Ultimate Guidebook* has chosen to award restaurants that have performed well above expectations. A seal of approval from the loudest voice on the island. To receive that prized title the restaurant has proven to be on the mark night after night, not just in the flavor and presentation of each dish, but in the overall experience of the customer, and it's a high honor that Sheri and I hoped to someday achieve.

I introduce myself and the man wonders if I'm the owner. I told him I was, and he said he thought so because the book said I might pay a visit to their table. I had no idea what he was talking about, so there was a beat of silence while I waited for him to expound. One of our write-ups might have referred to that, but I couldn't remember at the time. The man smiles and tells me they're here because of the guidebook, and he taps a long finger on the thick paperback. Good job, he says. I tell him thank you, but I think you're mistaken, we are not in there yet. I mentioned that we keep the ninth edition behind the bar in case anyone is looking for information and I know we're not in there.

Since the cover never changes, he directs my attention to the top where it reads tenth edition and my breath catches. Before I could stop myself, I snatched the copy off the table, my fingers betraying how greedy they were as I pawed my way to the South Shore Dining section. Meanwhile, he's thanking me for how good the food was, and telling me he wasn't surprised that we had received an 'ono' rating. I looked up incredulous.

Back to the book, I find the review on page two thirty-seven right at the bottom, and sure enough, there's a clearly stamped *'ono'* right next to it. I can't believe what I'm seeing, the write-up is glow-ing. In a moment of unguarded emotion, I tell them thank you again and excuse myself. As I pass the bar, I tell Sheri I'm heading to Costco and say nothing of the guidebook. There are things we need certainly, but it's now become the only reason I'm going, to buy ten copies of that book.

When I return, I've already read the passage about fifty times, so I could recite it flawlessly if called upon. For all we had managed to find our way through so far, this ranked as one of the proudest moments of my life. I called Sheri outside, and when she arrived, my excitement was hard to conceal as I handed her a book off the pile.

She knew immediately and her hands deftly shuffled through the pages like a Vegas card shark, smoothly spinning past entire sections before I could even give her the page number. I didn't bother. I wanted her to find it for herself and have the experience that I did. When she found it, she lit up from the inside, and we held each other for a few quiet minutes. The work would continue, all the hours still needed to push our vision forward would still consume our lives, this was in no way going to change that. We never once entertained the thought that we had 'arrived', but we proved, on that day, that we not only belonged in the restaurant business, we were being recognized for our efforts. The distinction and importance here in the islands, of receiving that 'ono' rating, was in the eyes of many, equal to the coveted Michelin Star award.

I'm proud to say we put together a place that people loved and wanted to come back to again and again. Whether it was a quick lunch before an afternoon excursion or a nightly mix of live music and dinner on the open lanais, Sheri and I were there. You could usually find us working our spots, her at the bar, and me bouncing between the prep room, the kitchen, and the stage. A night at the restaurant required me to wear many hats, but my favorite was the gray Stetson I slid low over my eyes when I sat in with the boys to sing a little country on Mondays.

We were so busy we had no time to go out and promote our restaurant, other than the radio ad, but somehow we were being noticed. The local paper ran two articles around the time we opened, and one of the entertainment guides did a small piece about our food. Even the food service industry took notice and interviewed our staff for a two-page spread in a magazine that would be read by our peers. A contributor to *Forbes,* who happened to be on vacation, was in on a Friday night and fell in love with the place. After Sheri spent an hour talking to him, he did a glowing write-up that appeared in the magazine the following month, and again the next month as he explored entrepreneurs in Hawaii.

The editor of our island newspaper called the restaurant to reserve a table near the stage for a Sunday evening. When he arrived, he sought out Sheri and introduced himself. He said he was there to do a story about Larry, accompanied by a few pictures. Larry Rivera was our standing Sunday entertainment. I had wandered up by this time, and after shaking hands, he asked me if he could snap a couple of photos during Larry's performance. I told him that would be fine, and he found his way to a table near the stage that our hostess had waiting for him.

About three-quarters of the way through Larry's set, while he was singing Kamalani I believe, the man came up to the bar where he found Sheri and I comfortably pulling beer taps, and mixing Mai Tai's. He said for once in his life he couldn't put into words the kind of time he was having. He wished he had brought his wife. He said he came in here to do an article on legendary Larry and found something he didn't expect. On and on he went, Sheri and I like two proud parents basking in the glow of this man in front of us.

After heaping on enough praise for the food, the service, and the restaurant in general to make me just a little uncomfortable, he wandered around to his point. He repeated what we already knew, that he was there to do a piece on Larry for the upcoming Fourth of July celebration, but would also love to do a review of the restaurant for the next edition at the same time. Would that be okay? Does the Pope wear a hat?

A few days later, Larry had a nice write-up in the Fourth of July insert, and the Garden Island Grille was featured on the front page of the business section. It was one of those surreal moments, sitting at one of our bar tables and reading what he had said about our restaurant, trying to grasp the fact that we were part of something worthy enough to be talked about around the island. He came into our restaurant seeking a treasure, and along with it, found a hidden gem.

Over a span of more than seventy years, Larry has continuously told people through his music, how much he loves Kauai. For most of that time, he was center stage at the famous Coco Palms resort. We have acquired a few left-over artifacts from that haven of recreation, and some of those items are casually spread throughout the restaurant. Few people even know what they are, random hallway signs and room numbers, weird light fixtures, and fake coconuts from a film shoot, but the unusual chairs that occupy just a couple of tables are another story.

With only weeks remaining before the restaurant opened, we found ourselves in a rented truck, bouncing on worn springs, as we navigated a small lane. We were lost somewhere behind the now-shuttered Coco Palms resort. Our destination was a disheveled and expectedly run-down edifice on the property, known as *The Coconut Palace*. We were given the opportunity to acquire a modicum of original cane chairs that occupied this once stately, and now beleaguered hall.

As we left the main road to follow this rutted and overgrown slash through a landscape of coconut trees, our minds were driven to a bygone era. We were immediately plunged into another time, one where people had yet to exist, and life as we know it seemed to evaporate. This sacred plain, now filled with soaring coconut trees, was the long-ago home of Kauai royalty known as the Ali'i, and the near presence of those wayward spirits was felt by both of us.

As the forest engulfed our vehicle, the canopy of leaves above darkened the sky and allowed only arrant shafts of sunlight to dance and skitter in the grove, adding a bit of enchantment to this odd mission. We slowly picked our way along the crumbling and weed-addled pavement of a walking path that has known the sandaled feet of erstwhile guests and celebrities from around the world. Midway through the campaign, I stopped the truck and shut off the engine. The only sound was the cooling tick of metal and the squeal of door hinges, as we slid out of our seats to become part of the quiet.

We stood rooted to the ground beneath our feet, reluctant to let go of the door or take a step beyond the vehicle for fear of intruding on this rare occurrence. We were listening to a stillness so deep and so reverent, that while the island bustled on around us, not a single note of humanity could ever be imagined. We stood there in awe until the silence was so overwhelming that we broke it upon whispers of wonder. With regret, we climbed back in and I re-filled the empty space with noise from the ignition.

We continued at a snail's pace to the end of the track, the decaying structure at last visible through the screen of vegetation. The man we were set up to meet with was already there and waiting for us. We tumbled from the truck with our earlier emotions still lingering, although we had now angled into the property so as to be near a road, and the sound of traffic filled the air. We went through the usual greetings and I tell him what an amazing place this is, and he agrees. At our own risk, we ventured inside.

Age and decay assaulted our senses as we moved farther into the vaulted space. At the front of the open room, looming in full view of everyone, is the main stage, sagging now and missing the steps necessary to reach it. The drapes and swags that formed the backdrop, once so gloriously vibrant and rich in color, were now hanging in moldy tatters. Directly in front of the stage is a warped and broken dance floor, the polished hardwood long ago turning soft and spongy with too much water and too many years. All of the windows were gone, their shattered glass adding to the ancient debris that now covered the floor. The roof has gaping holes, punched through by some giant fist, blue sky visible through the openings, and in the back, the cocktail bar and kitchen had fallen in on themselves.

It's been nearly thirty years since the record-setting winds and rain of hurricane Iniki devastated the island of Kauai, and shut down the beautiful Coco Palms forever. In the intervening decades since that fateful day, the jungle has been busy reclaiming its territory. The mystic lagoons, which sparkled and shimmered under a tropical sun for so many years and for so many people, are now green with algae, stagnant, and littered with rotting coconuts.

Every night, as the guests were seated for dinner in the open dining room, the long-held Coco Palms tradition of the torch lighting ceremony would begin. From somewhere, a drum would beat, and a scripted oration followed, with the presenter speaking in bold tones, as a chaotic and well-orchestrated run around the lagoons commenced. Hawaiian boys dressed in the ancient idea would race along the footpaths surrounding the moonlit pools, swinging a lighted stick. The pounding of their strides and the whirling of the flame were perfectly timed to light the one-hundred oil pots that lined the walkways, as each torch lighter passed in a blur. From anywhere you stood, watching the darkness light up with fire was spectacular.

I was pulled from the nostalgia that being there brings by the man's voice telling us that vandals had stolen the Koa wood doors and broke the twelve-foot, all-glass, ocean life mural behind the bar trying to get it off the wall. Looking around I could see that there was destruction beyond the type caused by time or the winds of a hurricane. Upon closer inspection, I could see that the sacrilege continued in the form of spray-painted graffiti, trash of every kind, and possible sleeping quarters. It was sad, like killing this once sparkling jewel of the island, over and over again. Because we knew the history of this special place, our hearts broke.

We spot our quarry huddled under a tarp in the corner of the room. Despite being more than sixty years old and left to their own survival, the cane chairs we selected for use in our restaurant were in excellent condition. As the three of us stood around the pile, running our hands along the smooth wood, the topic of who might have occupied those chairs was passed around. This was, after all, the very place where the legendary Larry Rivera had been center stage.

"From Elvis to Bing, to Frank Sinatra, they all came to see my show. I tell people, I didn't sing with Elvis, he sang with me. I didn't play with Bing, he played in my band." Larry would announce this to his rapt audience for decades after. With that line in my head from one of his shows, I look over to the decrepit stage, now glowing with more color and life than it should have, and I see Larry Rivera and his band commanding the room.

We knew from history that Larry was *the* music of the Coco Palms for more than thirty-five years. His voice was well known, from the dining room to the Flame room, to right here on this glorious stage, but to stand in this place and feel what it must have been like to be there, was awesome. Even in its current rundown state, you couldn't help but feel an energy and a past coming alive. Larry Rivera, in his flawless appearance, sharing a microphone and a friendship with the great Elvis Presley.

With the blow of a conch shell and the strum of a well-tuned ukulele, he was completely at home, giving throngs of mai-tai hoisting vacationers a little glimpse of old Hawaii. When the hotel closed permanently after hurricane Iniki, Larry found himself entertaining that same happy crowd all over the island.

He was born to be on stage and he loves to entertain people. He's cut from that rare and dwindling cloth of musicians who knows how to put on a show. Over the years he's tailored his act to fit him perfectly, the order of every song is arranged from first to last, and every ceremony is memorized and delivered with respect, honor, and power. The torch lighting, the hula, the lauding of the Coco Palms, and the tributes to this great island are expressed in his music, with a passion that leaves you breathless.

Dressed all in white, from his shoes to his collar, and wearing a red lei around his neck, he's a throwback to the days of Elvis in Blue Hawaii. And that's why he does it, to honor the memory of a man he spent so much time with. In Elvis he found a friend, a fellow bandmate, and a man who fell in love with one of his songs, bringing it to the big stage.

From the moment he landed to film Blue Hawaii at the Coco Palms, Elvis fell in love with Kauai and made it a part of his life until his passing. During those spur-of-the-moment trips, he would sit in with Larry and his band, and steal the show. A friendship outside of show business had begun, and Larry relates on stage, story after story of his life with the King.

I sometimes forget, with all his boundless energy and quick-witted personality, that Larry is approaching ninety and still doing everything he did when he was forty. The man defies logic. He's also become a great friend and more than that, he and his wife Gloria have become part of our extended family. He's the only musician I ever had that never missed a set, and every week he starts exactly on time. Twice a year he and his wife go to Vegas, which Larry insists that I know about months in advance, with bi-weekly reminders.

I remember the first time I met Larry, and the feeling of pride I had when I shook his hand and welcomed him to our restaurant while showing him to the stage. His eyes lit up when he saw the tiki hut that he would perform from. We had been open just four months and things were starting to finally make sense. I had put together a weekly line-up that featured an array of talented musicians from around the island, but I had trouble with Sunday nights for some reason. Larry changed all that.

I was working the kitchen one afternoon, Sheri was behind the bar re-stocking when I spotted a friend of ours reclining against the railing to the garden, enjoying the late afternoon. The stage was lit and ready for the duo that was playing that night to stumble through the back gate and start setting up. The music starts at six, so it was still a little early for that. Several tables were occupied and a couple was sitting at the bar trying to guess the titles of each song that came up on our playlist. Currently, Jimmy Buffett was lamenting the fact that he was a pirate, born two hundred years too late, just an over forty victim of fate, and while they couldn't come up with the name of the song, they still agreed that he hadn't missed his calling.

Since the day we put this thing in motion, rather than elevate one item on our menu, we decided on music as our signature dish. Our idea was to showcase great local talent, not just on the weekends, or some special occasion, but every night of the week. In our discussions, Larry's name would come up often, and we would ruminate on what it would mean to us to have him on our stage. The same questions would swirl: What would it take to get him? Could we get him? Would he even consider the offer? Furthermore, we had no way of reaching out to him, and to date, had scarcely met anyone who could.

The good news was that one of the people who could accomplish that had just strolled into the restaurant and was now standing at the rail to the courtyard, relaxing with a pint of Longboard in the waning sunlight. I knew from the beginning that I wanted Larry on the Aloha Stage, at least once, but at present, I had no time to fully invest in the chase. Reluctantly, I was about to make a foray into that pursuit, and ask a favor from a new friend.

The man quietly gazing out over the garden and looking toward the stage was, in fact, a fellow restaurant owner and businessman here on Kauai, and had known Larry for a long time. We had met him a few months after arriving on the island and we've stayed in touch ever since, although I was never comfortable bringing up his relationship with Larry in regard to him performing at the restaurant. That was about to change.

"Hey, listen, I'm hoping you might be willing to do me a small favor." I said after joining him at the rail.

"I can try, what is it before I say yes?"

"Well, I would love to see Mr. Coco Palms on my stage someday, But I have no idea how to make that happen, and I'm betting maybe you do. Could you give me his number and I can reach out?" I said.

"I was just admiring the stage and thinking the same thing, but I can't give out his number without asking him, I'm sorry." He looked around, as if seeing the courtyard for the first time, and added, "I'm sure he would love to play here, I just don't feel comfortable. I'll see him this week and I can ask him to call you if that's okay"

"Yeah, of course it's okay, thank you, I can't tell you how much this means to me, and the restaurant."

I shook his hand and walked back into the kitchen. A little while later he grabs me to say goodbye and tells me that he just got off the phone with Larry.

"He was returning my call about an event we have coming up and I mentioned your restaurant. He seemed interested and wanted your phone number."

"Wow, I assume you gave it to him? Did he say if he has any nights open?" I said, surprised.

"He wanted me to ask you about tomorrow night, Sundays are good for him but I told him to just call you and you guys can work it out."

"No shit." I said.

I thanked him again as we walked toward the exit. I stood outside in the sunshine thinking about what had just taken place, and wondering if I would actually hear from Larry.

For a guy like Larry Rivera, you make an opening, but it just so happened that Sunday had been the hardest to fill, so it was the one night that was open the most. Whenever a Sunday would come around that I didn't have anyone to perform on the stage, Kona Jones, our Tuesday musician, was always more than happy to fill in.

After fumbling through my conversation with Larry and setting up the following night, we turned our attention toward getting the word out. We put signs up all over town as well as in front of the restaurant. We tapped one of our employees to handle social media and Lee quickly put together a high-quality radio spot, which ran all day Sunday. Those things seemed to be our quickest, and best ways to announce that Larry Rivera, "Mr. Coco Palms", would be live at the Garden Island Grille that night.

We had a full house and then some, the entire staff was hustling, including Sheri and I. His music and his stories would come to me in snatches and snippets as I worked to make everyone else's night unforgettable. The ironic part of the whole thing was that we wanted Larry for so long, performing on our stage, but we had no time to enjoy his show. In what appeared to be the blink of an eye, it was eight o'clock, and his set was over. I look to the stage in the courtyard and see him packing up his gear, stowing away the ukulele. We had missed it.

For a brief moment, a form of despair clung to me. Dark, swirling clouds of poor me. I shook it off. This night wasn't for me, or Sheri, it was for them, and they loved it. I stood next to Sheri, who was saying goodbye to people as they passed by the bar, laughing and commenting, and we both knew that even though we hosted it, we had missed something special, something that may never be repeated.

When Larry walked in the back door after loading up his stuff, he was all smiles and splendid white. I greeted him with a hug and told him how great it was. If I were to look at the night in its proper perspective, in what ultimately mattered, everything went off flawlessly, and as a restaurant, we made a killing. We also added a bit of promotion to our name, but somehow, the idea of not being a spectator seemed so much more important. He remarked on how busy it had gotten through the night and how much fun he had. He said the tiki stage made him feel like he was back in the Flame Room.

As he made his way out the back door to his car, we walked along with him, happy to be in the presence of someone we'd heard and read so much about, a man who spent his entire life living his dream. When we reached his vehicle, Sheri and I were both there to thank him again and say goodbye to his wife. I was trying to figure out how to tease out another date from him without looking too pushy, or needy, and running through my mind how I might approach it, when Larry, like it was written in stone, turned to me and solved my dilemma.

"Listen, I'm going to Vegas for the Super Bowl next week. I apologize for the short notice, but the following Sunday I'll be here, and I'll let you know when I go again."

"Okay. So…. what are you saying, you want to come back every Sunday? You want to make this a regular gig?" I was surprised.

"Well, not next week, I said I'd be in Vegas, but yeah, I wouldn't turn this down. I thought you wanted someone every week. I've got to be honest. Until I got here, I was thinking this was a one-time show, but you guys are wonderful and I love the stage. What, you don't want every week?"

"No, no, no, every week was exactly what we were hoping for, but we weren't sure with your schedule…."

"It's no problem, I'll see you in two weeks."

And with that, he was gone, and Sheri and I looked at each other stunned. Sunday nights turned out to be an experience few will ever forget; I know I won't.

## CHAPTER 17

# Napoleon steals the show

On a warm, late August night, in what would unknowingly become our final year, I stood on the Aloha Stage in the courtyard of the Garden Island Grille, with a chef coat draped over my right arm, and our fabulous one-legged Filipino dishwasher squirming under my left. It took a good deal of coaxing to get him out there. He'll dance up a storm in front of the bar in his apron, turning on the whole restaurant, but he doesn't like to be pinned down.

What I had planned that night had come together perfectly, and Napoleon, as he always does, was pretending to be embarrassed by the applause of the full restaurant. I let him go so he could get back to work and out of the spotlight, as that seemed to be his immediate concern, and he limped off back to the dish room having received his reward, with an animated wave.

Just over a year and a half before, he had carried that same limp through the back door of the restaurant for the first time, with the same vitality. Through his broken English and Filipino pidgin, and letters that he can't pronounce, I gathered that he was not happy with his current employer, and wanted a job washing dishes.

I could see that he walked a little crooked, so I pointed, and asked him if he was okay. Without shame he hiked up his pant leg, exposing a gleaming steel prosthetic, which he slapped with the palm of his hand. 'Accident' he said, and began pleading with me that it was no problem, that he was a hard worker and could do his job, and on and on. Because of his broken English, most of what he said I failed to understand. There were a lot of hand gestures, and some pantomiming of what he was trying to say, not for my benefit as I would learn through time, but because he was so naturally expressive.

I hired him, and he was so happy he couldn't thank me enough or stop running his hand up and down the sleeve of the coat I was wearing, as I had come from the kitchen to meet him.

"Tank you, Dabe. I start now?" He can't pronounce the letter *v* or *f*, and the *th* sound seems to be too many letters, so out goes the *h*. It was a process, learning his language, not his native Tagalog, but the language of Napoleon.

"No, not now, Thursday at three."

"Okay, I start now, tursday, good dis one."

I also learned over time that when Napoleon says 'now' it means whatever time I told him to be somewhere. There was confusion over this once, or twice until I finally figured it out. His way of speaking, likely resulting from the accident he was in, had me searching out a translator more often than not, usually one of my cooks who knew him well. His Ilocano and Tagalog were flawless, but he had lost his fluent English.

As it turned out for Sheri and I, Napoleon was one of our greatest finds. In the beginning, I had no idea what to expect from him as far as work went. I knew he would at least show up, or thought I did, but could he hold up for a full shift, washing dishes, scrubbing pans, and running clean plates to the kitchen all night? Couple the wooden leg, as he called it, with the fact that he was pushing sixty, and I wasn't completely sure how this would go. But from the moment we met him, his personality and exuberance demanded that we hire him.

Within a week he had erased any doubts I might have had and we worked out a comfortable schedule. He settled in and began shedding any signs of shyness that was evident in his first couple of nights. He captured the restaurant when he would come out, still clad in his plastic apron, and dance in front of the bar. He knew everything from disco, to hula, and his steps took him to wherever the music led. Coming out of his shell would be a drastic understatement to describe the Napoleon I had met a few years ago, to the one who has emerged since.

Our restaurant has always had a good vibe, but at night when the music is taking center stage and every table is full, there's a buzz in the air and an energy that moves through the place you can almost touch, like crackling ozone. There is movement everywhere. Servers and food runners bustling around, people coming and going, the musicians in full swing, and the guests themselves, all in motion. No longer just eating and drinking, but legs bouncing under tables, and heads bobbing above.

In the middle of all this, Napoleon shuffles out of the back and starts dancing like he's auditioning for Broadway, and the dynamic of the restaurant changes. Tables begin interacting with each other, laughing together, and pulling out cameras because what's taking place is too bizarre not to be documented.

I've been to a lot of restaurants with a lot of cool themes, one even had a hurricane sweep through about every hour, but I've never seen the dishwasher, clad in full apron no less, come out dancing the salsa and energize the entire crowd, but that was Napoleon. Without any words, he had the ability to bring together, if only for a moment, couples and families who otherwise thought they were going out for a simple dinner.

I've been around Napoleon long enough now to know that the day-to-day isn't easy, that in the previous decade his life was forever altered in the blink of an eye, and the man that once was, is no more. Yet, he spins gold from the difficulties he has faced, for him every day is a new offering, and he expects to share it with everyone. The accident that shattered his former life allowed him to touch ours, and while he may not be our most gifted employee, he burns the brightest.

A year later, and a few months into his reign as the heart of the restaurant, Napoleon started commenting about the kitchen, and specifically the chefs. I was still, at this time, struggling to understand everything he said, so when it didn't seem like the guys in the kitchen were a problem, I let it go. I told Sheri that I think Napoleon is trying to tell me that he wants to be a cook, and I don't know how to tell him that I can't put him there.

For one thing, I didn't have an opening at the time, at least not for a shift that I felt comfortable putting him in. Secondly, and probably the most delicate, was that I didn't think he could handle the pressure, let alone all the duties that the job required. But I couldn't tell him that, and it broke my heart more than it would his, so I tried to wait him out, hoping he would forget it. No dice.

A month, or more, would slip by without a mention, and then he'd be back, asking me about the kitchen in that round-a-bout way of his. As a last effort, I told him that his job was important, and he did it so well that if I moved him to the kitchen, I would need two guys to fill his old spot. Besides, as a cook, you'd be too busy to dance.

Although my ear had become better tuned to his mixed bag of speech, I still required interpretation from time to time. But, for his part, he usually understood the things I would tell him, so I was surprised to see a look of confusion cross his face. I found it ironic that I had somehow turned the tables, and it was Napoleon, not me, who stood there looking puzzled.

Before he turned away, I had caught a look of disappointment mingled in, maybe even shades of sadness, that clouded his otherwise bright eyes. When I thought back, that look accompanied those eyes every time we had this conversation. I felt bad, that for all he meant to us, I was denying him something he continued asking for, and seemed to really want, but we had a business to run, and for it to have a chance to perform in a well-oiled state, I needed the right people in the right place. It turned out that I couldn't have been more wrong in reading the situation.

After work one night, Jeric, our multi-talented lead cook, pulled me aside and said he wanted to talk to me about Napoleon. Jeric had been renting a room from Napoleon and his wife for the past six months and he took it upon himself to look out for him. Both of them, being from the Philippines, shared Tagalog as their native language and a bond was easily formed between them.

Jeric knew as well as I did that Napoleon would not be able to stand up to the rigorous demand of a kitchen schedule and everything that went with it. He was a perfect fit for our restaurant where he was, and he seemed to flourish there. I told Jeric all these things before he even started talking, finishing with I can't do it, I wish I could, but I just can't.

His smile broadened into an uncomfortable laugh, which I had learned from previous experience meant he had something on his mind, however, shame rendered him unable to say it. It was getting late and I was growing a little irritated by the whole charade, so I told him to stop laughing and tell me what the hell is going on, what am I missing.

"Boss," he said, eyes cast to the table below our drinks, looking at every nuance of the four-foot circle as though it contained his speech. I waited somewhat impatiently for him to continue, already knowing how this conversation would end.

He went on to tell me in his sheepish way, that what Napoleon wants is a chef coat, but he's too ashamed to ask you. He thought if he could work in the kitchen, he could get one that way. I was caught off guard. Any rebuttal I was preparing to counter what I expected to hear, such as Jeric's normally sound plea that he would personally train Napoleon, suddenly lost its shape and disappeared on my lips.

I recovered and instead asked him what he was talking about. I thought he wanted you to ask me about the kitchen. No, he said, he wanted me to ask you about a chef coat, he doesn't want to work in there, he just wants to be one of us.

Clarity was dawning and the whole thing was starting to make a lot more sense. Napoleon tugging at the sleeve of the coat I wore, feeling the fabric. His outright excitement every time I switched out the old, battered coats, with crisp, clean new ones, telling each chef how handsome they looked. He wore his feelings and his emotions right out there for all to see, and now I could see them too.

"Well, if all he wants is a chef coat," I said, "I can do that. I can defiantly do that."

I leaned back in my chair to see Napoleon eyeing our conversation from two tables away, a look of concern etching his features. When he saw me, an enormous grin split his face, and two thumbs shot into the air.

"Can?" he said.

I replied with my own bewildered smile and gave him back two thumbs up.

"Can."

As that little piece of drama was quietly playing along in the background of the previous year, Napoleon began to shed small flickers of light on the accident that had forever changed his life. Every couple of weeks, with a drink in front of him at the end of the night, he would confide to Sheri and me about the circumstances surrounding his missing leg. Over the course of several months, mixed in with a variety of other escapades from his life, Napoleon told us his story, in his own way, and in its own order.

He began by laying out his past, how he was born and raised in the Philippines, and traveled to Saudi Arabia for work, which he found in the palace of a Prince. Wild, animated stories, told the way only Napoleon can tell them, would emerge regularly from those years spent baking in the desert. Little by little he shared his life and his extraordinary tale of courage and survival.

As my mind gathered up all these memories and moments of Napoleon's unique life, I stepped back to the present, where I was on stage to relate his story of loss and redemption, and to show respect and honor to a very humble man.

Before the duo that was playing that night got started, I informed them that I was hi-jacking part of their show to make a presentation. Halfway through their set, after I had joined them for a couple of songs, they dutifully laid down their instruments and somehow managed to hold themselves in line. If you know any musicians, then you know they're always tuning, picking, fiddling, or check, checkin' the microphone. They surprisingly did none of that.

I stood there while the happy crowd finished their applause, gathering my thoughts. As excited as I was to be in front of them, telling a story about our dishwasher and offering him a gift, I was a little uneasy about how the tables would respond to a break in the music. This was a bit unusual for us. While I waited I couldn't help but think back over the last few years. It's amazing what goes through your mind in just a few seconds. Looking around and meeting the eyes of people who I know love our restaurant, memories of what brought us to this point, flickered through my brain.

We had experienced so much. For a while, every day was another wild ride, but through it all, we learned and grew, and became a place that people depended on, a place where the atmosphere was unlike anywhere they have ever been. A place where they knew the owners because the owners were part of the staff.

Even with all the long hours and hard work we still managed to have a lot of fun, and we met a lot of great people from all over the world. We have guests that immediately fall in love with the restaurant who we will see multiple times on their ten-day vacation. We have others that wander in on their last night and by the end, they're telling Sheri that it's too bad they spent so much time on the north shore, they should have been here every night.

So often, Sheri will engage with a couple at the bar, in for a quick drink before their reservation at one of the up-scale places that offer sunsets, and eighty-dollar steaks. Between the story she is telling and the electricity that is buzzing around with the band setting up, they cancel the reservation and spend the whole night where they are, eating fish tacos. Everyone around them is making them feel like family.

Brock and Eve, our friends from Canada, were so taken by the restaurant and the atmosphere around them that it became their home away from home for three months a year. Literally. I'd walk into the prep room and find Eve plating desserts or making salads, or Brock, helping Sheri change the Bikini Blonde keg. Of course, he likely finished the barrel and was hurrying the process for another pint, but it was still helpful. Through the years, our friendship has grown, and they have developed relationships with some of our staff, keeping in touch with them even long after they were back in Canada. Napoleon puts Brock on facetime at least once a week, even though I keep reminding him, to no avail, that it's already midnight where they live. He just laughs.

On a recent visit, they were married at our restaurant on the Aloha Stage. We've had so many great nights surrounding the entertainment in that courtyard, but this was by far the most beautiful. The whole place was brightly decorated for the occasion, and the stage was transformed into a wedding altar. They asked us not to close for the ceremony, so it became a blend of family, friends, and people looking for a night out, that throughout the evening, became one group, and had a time I'm sure they won't forget. It's not every day that a casual dinner reservation finds you front and center for a Hawaiian-style wedding and the celebration that follows.

I was again brought back to the present by the overwhelming silence that surrounded me. The rattling of pans from the kitchen and the whirling of the blender from behind the bar were the only sounds. The story I was about to tell concerned a man who brought something unexpected, not just into the restaurant, but into our lives, and whose mere presence among us is the telling of its own miracle. He's not a saint, and he's not above a good scolding, but Napoleon brings some swagger and dedication, and a strength of character that is rarely seen.

I had it in my mind to do more than just hand Napoleon a chef coat. I could have done that weeks before, during pau hana with our staff. I wanted to honor him, not as one employee over another, but because of the second chance he was given, because he didn't waste the rest of his life in sorrow and self-pity. Instead, he took what life gave him and faced it head-on, and in the process, he quietly impacted everyone he met on that road.

I found myself looking from table to table and I realized that staring back at me were couples and families that had made our restaurant a part of their lives, and a necessary part of their yearly vacation to Kauai, for as long as we've been open. While the weekends are always busy, by simple chance that Friday night, both dining rooms were full of people who had become friends of the restaurant over the years. Visitors and locals alike, faces and names I recognized were occupying the open lanais. At the bar sat a group of our Friday night regulars, unwinding after a long week.

I introduced myself for the benefit of those that didn't know me, most did, and I thanked everyone for being there. I launched into what I was in front of them to say. When I began telling them that I was here to talk about Napoleon, our night dishwasher, and present him with a small gift, heads instinctively turned to the back, toward the dish room where Napoleon kept his office. If you've been to our restaurant fifty times, or only once, you quickly learn who Napoleon is, and you expect him to come bouncing out of the back, apron swishing around his legs, dancing to whatever moves him when the band is playing.

After a brief outline of the man, and an explanation of why I was giving a chef's coat to a dishwasher, that he was becoming part of an elite group, I paused for a few seconds, thinking. Not about if I should continue, Napoleon had already given me the go-ahead on that, but how, because I didn't even know if I knew the whole story, or to tell the truth, understood it. I pressed on.

Napoleon had spent his life in strange, far-away places and when he finally settled in California, he married late. As he approached his fortieth year, a trip to the Philippines was in the works. It would be a time to reunite with his family, but his wife was unable to go, so with her blessing, he made the trip alone. As he traveled the many miles from the airport in Manilla to his province in the hills, the bus in which he was riding missed a turn in the dark. After smashing through a guardrail, it tumbled hundreds of feet down a steep embankment, coming to rest on its side.

Up to that point, the ride had been uneventful. While enduring the long commute and cramped quarters, he was wedged in next to a young girl about twelve, her family somewhere among the throng of passengers. Being Napoleon, he carried on a conversation with her in Tagalog for most of the long ride, learning that her mother and father were a few rows back, the family had been separated as too many passengers squeezed into tight spaces and jammed up the aisle. He told her about his own family, there in the Philippines, and spoke of his wife in California.

There was a comfortable silence between questions and answers, as the over-crowded and over-burdened bus, rocked and swayed to its destiny. The young girl somehow knew that there was nothing to fear from this open-hearted stranger. Suddenly, they were both lunging forward, Napoleon instinctively reaching out to restrain the young girl, as the scream of air brakes and squealing of tires filled the air.

The bus slouched sideways as the right wheels left the pavement and sought purchase on the soft shoulder. Skidding and careening, now out of control, it slammed through a wooden guardrail, pieces whickering through the air and crashing through the windshield, instantly killing the driver. Napoleon was clutching the back of the seat in front of him with all he had, while still trying to restrain the girl and understand what was going on. He was terrified.

It all happened so quickly that before he could process what was taking place, the bus was sliding down a sixty-degree embankment, and chaos had erupted. People were screaming, bodies were flying, and windows were exploding. Suitcases and trunks, piled too high and tied haphazardly to the roof, broke free and rocketed down the steep hillside ahead of the screaming behemoth. Near the end of its unconventional, terrifying descent, the bus rolled three times and came to rest on its side.

In the wake of the disaster lay a cliffside strewn with bodies and debris. Napoleon had lost consciousness, his head and body battered, and his leg crushed amid the wreckage. He would much later learn that the young girl in the seat next to him, the one he told story after story to and hopelessly tried to protect in the early moments of the crash, had not survived, her name, along with her parents, listed with so many others. More than his own frightening memories of that night, her death still haunts him the most.

After finally being rescued, he was declared dead twice and managed to fight his way back. In those moments he claims to have been standing in brilliance, like the sparkling of a flawless diamond, a light that seemed to emanate from everywhere, soft and radiant. Each time, a voice he described as belonging to his mother, would urge him to go no further, proclaiming that it wasn't his time. He was propelled backward with the force of her words, and the dazzling light receded as he re-joined our world.

He would emerge from this with new challenges and his own understanding of how fragile and fleeting life is. He never let that night defeat him, or in any way cast a shadow over what remained, in fact, his outlook, always so sunny, betrays the myriad of afflictions that have become his constant companion. In the aftermath of the accident, Napoleon suffered multiple fractures and broken bones, he lost his right leg above the knee, a kidney, his spleen, several teeth, a little bit of hearing, and some brain tissue. For as long as it took to patch him up, the healing will go on forever.

Back on stage, it was so quiet you could hear a pin drop, and I was fighting emotion through the whole thing. I could see many who felt the same way, having at one time or another, an encounter with our fabled dishwasher. Whether it was a gentleman on his way to the restroom that Napoleon engaged in a quick disco, or ladies of all ages trying to keep up with his tango, or just a simple high five, he made you feel good and he made our guests feel good. Sheri and I were routinely asked more about Napoleon, is he here, can we get a picture, when will he dance, than any musician we put on stage, and we have some good ones.

I finished the presentation by saying that I didn't know Napoleon before the accident, but the man Sheri and I know now, we wouldn't trade for any version. I told them that he had been angling for a position in the kitchen, but since those spots were filled, we created a new title for him and a small gift to go with it.

When I had finally secured Napoleon next to me on the stage, I was held in place by the outpouring of emotion that our guests were showing to a man that had in some way touched, and maybe inspired them. I offered up what was in my hand. I presented him with a royal blue chef coat, the Garden Island Grille, and his full name, Napoleon Villanueva, stitched in gold above the left side pocket. The exact coat all of our chefs and cooks wear. Almost. Under his name, I had added a third line announcing his new title, Executive Dishwasher. And yes, there were perks. We now, quite possibly, had the first and only executive dishwasher on the island. Hell, maybe the only one in the world.

## CHAPTER 18

# Where do we go from here?

The images and emotions of that last story brought me swimming back to where I was, sitting at the table with Randy, who had finished a cheeseburger and was listening intently. It's hard to believe that I gave Napoleon that coat only six months ago, and now, where do we go from here? I looked down in front of me and somewhere during my tale a Jameson had appeared. Grateful, I took a long swallow and sat there wrung out. I was drained, not only from the effort of talking but from the effort of holding back the stress of the last few days. Just talking about something else felt like a relief.

After consulting my cell phone, I discovered that I had been talking for over an hour. What started as a whim soon turned into some kind of therapy, with me on the couch.

"You know, that's the longest, I think, that anyone has ever sat and talked to me, that was awesome man, thank you." He said.

"I didn't realize that I was going on so long, I'm sorry about that. I guess it felt good to talk about something different." I admitted.

"I know, I get it man. We keep hearing about this Covid thing, and now we're all worried that we'll get it and will we live, and the whole thing reeks of conspiracy. It's scary."

"That is a concern for sure, but how about what it will do to all of these businesses that are closing right now? How many will be able to come back? Will we be able to come back? It's expensive you know, to shut down indefinitely and then re-open again. To what, an uncertain future?" I said.

"I don't know man, I'm not sure what to do. I guess we all have something to think about. I'll probably lay low and hide out in my apartment. I've got a pretty good stockpile of stuff I need." He said, and I wasn't surprised.

"What do you mean, hide out? How do you hide from a virus?" I was trying to be serious. It was so Randy.

"I don't know, but I've got a lot to think about. Thank you for trying to help me, for taking the time to just sit here and let me listen. I'm staying away from people, so you won't see me for a while." He explained, as he retreated from his chair and stood to leave.

"Well, I hope you really think about the life you want to live and the people you want in it. I'd love to see you in a better place, but you have to want that. I can't change your life, only you can do that. I think if you would at least take a step toward being a part of something, begin your own process of re-connecting with even one person, you'll find your life moving in a better direction. You've got a lot to offer, Randy. Seeing how all this news has affected you, it could be your chance to start over. Make the rest of your life whatever you want it to be. If you're honest with yourself, the one you're living isn't it." I was really hoping that I had struck a chord.

"It's not as easy as you make it sound, sometimes I feel like I am who I am, and nothing can change that." He said.

"When my mother died, it changed the direction of my life. Her sudden departure pushed me into the life I had waiting for me. I've grown more as a person in the last five years than I have in the two decades prior to it. You're right when you say you are who you are. But that doesn't mean you can't change. I think that after seeing you today, you're still searching for who you are and this might be the opportunity to find out who that really is. It's time to take back control, Randy."

"I don't take advice well, but you're right. You've held up a pretty big mirror and I don't like what I see. I think I've come to realize that I want that change, I just can't do it here. I guess I've got a phone call from my mother to return. I need to make amends for the man I've been, for the son I've been."

He surprised me by putting out his hand. I didn't hesitate when I took it and gave it a shake with both of mine.

"Hope to see you around," I said.

"Maybe, but I don't think so." He replied.

And with that he turned on his heel and strode out the door, trailing hope for the future in his wake. I stayed where I was, for the time being, certain I would see him again, and thought about what had transpired over the previous couple of weeks, and what it would mean for our own future. My wife joined me with the guest book in hand and occupied the seat across from me that Randy had just vacated, and together we quietly took it all in. There were no reservations for the evening, nor would there be for many to come.

We were closing early, and now that the day was winding down, I could feel the effects that the strain of the last week had left behind. I was mentally and emotionally drained, and I knew Sheri

was too. The winter tourist season had gone well beyond expectations this year. The island had started getting busy a week before
Christmas and had continued to build momentum all through the
winter. In fact, we were coming off one of the biggest weeks we have
ever had. Even amid the escalating news of the Coronavirus and
the frenzy it was causing on the mainland.

We talked a little bit, Sheri and I, while the crew did their
clean-up. We both have our own closing duties every night, but for
now, those things could wait. It was enough to just sit there and
watch, probably for the last time. The Governor had spoken a few
days before, the Covid19 lockdown had reached Kauai.

Scores of memories were everywhere. I looked into the
corner of the courtyard, where the tree that produced our tangerine margaritas was once again promising a good time. I thought
about the local guy who tried to sell me a small armload that he had
picked from that tree when he thought no one was looking. They
were. I bought them anyway. Good, bad, most of them random, but
all those memories were vying for my attention, as names, faces,
and moments beset my mind. There isn't a place, or a corner in that
restaurant that I can look to, and not find one.

As my eyes took in the rest of the garden where the stage
is located, they settled on the basil and I couldn't help but smile
thinking about Robert, or Jeric, looking every bit the part in their
spotless coats, making a show of snipping those fresh herbs in front
of the entire restaurant. Everything we made, from the fresh fruit
juices in our drinks at the bar, to the herbs and vegetables that went
into every dish, was put together with the highest quality in mind,
and this little bit of showmanship was the embodiment of that.

The Aloha Stage, so alive over the years with lights and color,
and music from around the island, now stood sullen and cheerless

in the weak light of the late afternoon. Just the thought of it brings excitement to my eyes. The sight of that oasis of light commanding the courtyard and the attention of every guest brings to memory all the music that was played on it. From legends like Uncle Kalani, and the great Larry Rivera, to up-and-coming talent getting their feet wet, we've seen almost every local musician the island has to offer.

Under a thatched roof held aloft by bamboo poles, twinkling blue lights bathe the floor in a soft glow from above, while colored spotlights enhance the aura that surrounds the scene. At the back of the stage, a lighted moon sets a track across Hanalei Bay, sparkling with the lunar reflection as it slowly dips behind the mountains known as Bali Hai. In large script letters, the word 'Aloha' stands out in three-dimension across the top, and in full view, burning with dazzling red lights.

The carpeted stage made me think about a day close to Christmas, when Byron, our Thursday musician, was on stage captivating the audience with the songs of Hawaiian myths and legends. His wife, in bare feet, was dramatizing the words to each, through an ancient dance, known as the hula. He had sprinkled holiday music into his mix that week, and as his final offering, gave us O' Holy Night, sung completely in Hawaiian. Amber, dressed in the colors of the season, and lost in the art of the dance, gave us the interpretation. The arrangement was so magical that everyone stopped what they were doing and just took it in. It was a moving experience, and together they left us with a memory that will live on forever.

The garden is the perfect setting for that wonderland of light and sound. Ensconced in tropical foliage and overhung with the branches of my coconut palm, the little grass and bamboo shack huddles in flawless symphony. It gave our restaurant an identity, and people would ask throughout the day who was playing, and when. Every night was a different experience, but they all flowed together to create the laid-back island theme we were reaching for. Once I found a line-up that fit the restaurant, the atmosphere emanating from that corner, took care of itself.

The cooks were back-and-forth, from the hot line to the dish room. I could hear them yelling 'hot pans' and Napoleon complaining about where they were putting them. Nothing unusual, but it made me think of Robert and how he started this whole thing. How everything we do from setting up in the morning to breaking down at night, even the shift change in the middle, was orchestrated and meticulously laid out by that great man. He brought a high level of comfort to our lives at a time when there was little to be found.

So many employees have come through these doors in the five years we've been open that it's hard to keep track of them all. We have five that started with us on day one, and they are who we lean on the most. Some are here a week, others a month or two before they move on, or I have to fire them. Several have stuck around a year, or more before something else takes them away. It's a transient business. I did hire a cook twice. He failed to show up for his first day on both occasions. You would think I couldn't possibly do it a third time. I did. Same results.

As I continued to sit there, I found myself increasingly unable to move. I was frozen in place by something I couldn't define. Shock. Disbelief maybe. Nostalgia was part of it, but that was born out of memories from a shattered dream. We had done well in this business. We weren't declaring bankruptcy, and we didn't owe our creditors or suppliers. In fact, we had run our restaurant well into the black and were consistently turning a nice profit. Yet, tomorrow our doors would be closed, and an uncertain future loomed in front of us.

To this point, Trip Advisor, Yelp, and Facebook had us consistently in the mid to upper four stars, and we were ranked higher than most of the restaurants on the island, including some high dollar, high market names. We received the Trip Advisor Certificate of Excellence every year we were open and the 'ono' rating in the tenth and eleventh editions of The Ultimate Kauai Guidebook. This dream we had built from scratch was finding success, and our hard work was finally paying off. We were proud of the staff we had come to know as family, and that group, with Sheri and I at the head, were moving the restaurant to a whole new level.

It was only a week ago that our good friend Dan stopped in for his usual Tuesday night. He's the General Manager of one of the large resorts on the island and occasionally my Wednesday golf partner. He was sitting at the bar nursing a Longboard and not looking too happy about it. It was busy for a Tuesday night, but I still managed to get a few words in with him. He didn't stay long, and what he told Sheri and me before he walked out the door, seemed at first, unfortunate. Only later would we fully comprehend the meaning of his words. He said he had just received cancelations for all his large groups and conferences through May, a loss of over two million dollars, and he looked shocked.

It took a day, or so, for events to finally register what it was that he had said to us, but when it did, his words were prophetic. It's not that we were slow to catch on. Or that we didn't understand the trend. We were middle-aged Americans, free to pursue the life of our choosing, raised in a country where the endless march of progress continues. It sounds naïve to say, but we lived our lives under the security of our great nation, and we never had a reason to entertain phrases like economic shutdown, or God forbid, global pandemic.

Yet, here we were. It took only two days for the President to mandate a limit to social gatherings, a number that would fall to zero before the weekend was over. Everything we knew began to grind to a halt. Playoffs were cut short, seasons abruptly ended, and every event possibly conceived was canceled. It's ironic in an age of bigger and more powerful bombs, that what finally brought the world to its knees, could only be viewed under a microscope. But then again, we're living in unprecedented times, at least for us, and life as we once knew it, looks to be changing forever.

I wrestled my mind from all these thoughts and looking around, found Sheri struggling with the same thing. Coming off the heels of everything shaking loose on the mainland, our governor, for good reason, announced a state-wide shutdown and quarantine through May, and possibly beyond. He mixed no words when he said visitors were not welcome, and he was closing the airports to incoming flights. Extra departures were added and tourists were leaving the islands and heading for their homes in droves.

Tourism drives the Hawaiian economy, so it was a formality when he said that the following day, all hotels, resorts, restaurants, and bars, would also close through May. Limited to take-out only. Here on Kauai that meant hundreds of businesses alone, and the ripple effect would take with it many more.

My thoughts kept swinging around to our employees. Most, if not all of them were working two, or three jobs, and still living paycheck to paycheck. In the coming days, thousands of people on this island would be unemployed. There wasn't anything anyone could do. It was mandated that all non-essential businesses close their doors for the foreseeable future.

We both reached our own conclusions at the same time and as the sun was setting, not just on the day, but on a chapter of our lives, we went back to work, to the things we had done night after night for the last five years. When the clean-up was done and the doors were closed to the public, we had planned a final gathering of our staff and friends for what was to be the last time in this magical spot. The next day was sure to bring new worries and fears for everyone, but for that night, for the first time in a long time, we would try not to look ahead.

What became the biggest coincidence in this short-lived but wild ride of the Garden Island Grille was that the pandemic and subsequent shutdown came together in the same month as our lease was expiring. After a conversation with the property owner revealed their plan for handling the shutdown, which was rumored to extend through the summer and beyond, we decided to roll the dice on our location and not renew our lease. Their plan was expectedly shaky and not well defined. They, like everyone else, were scrambling for solutions to a problem no one was prepared for. The consensus seemed to be an unwavering business-as-usual approach. We would make up the loss on the back end of a new lease.

We had entertained other lease offers and looked at other locations over the previous month just to see what was out there, but in the end, it seemed likely that we would stay where we were and come to terms at the end of the month. Now, with our current lease ending, and the island effectively closed, it didn't make sense to sign another one and make a commitment that would be impossible to fulfill. I didn't need to be an Einstein to add that up.

The day before, we took the time to quietly announce to our employees that when the island finally lifted its ban on tourism, we would not be re-opening in the same location, if at all. With so much uncertainty swirling around everything that we so easily took for granted, we knew that the staff needed a night to pose their questions and vent their fears. I think maybe we did too. We had no idea what the future would ultimately hold for us, whether we would open again somewhere else, or if the winds would continue to blow, taking us in another direction.

All we knew for sure was that tonight would belong to our staff and our incredible group of friends that had made the restaurant so special over the years. In a few short hours, we would be laughing, crying, toasting, and paying homage to what had become our home since we opened the doors. The mix of people that would soon fill the room represented the entirety of our closest friends, so they knew that this night would be the final gathering, the end of pau hana, and the last dance of the Garden Island Grille. They also knew that as much as that restaurant meant to them, it was everything to us.

For the last five years, our lives had run at full throttle, and although we set high standards for our restaurant, the demands we put on our employees were far less than what we put on ourselves. It's taken us all this time to figure out what we were doing and how to do it better, but we were in the process of looking beyond. We had weathered all that this business could throw at us in a climate that was foreign in every way, and every day we beat it back, every day we proved another stat wrong.

But not this time. Then again, this time is altogether different. This time we've conceded the battle until it can be fought on level ground. If or when this all ends, how long will it take to get back to what we once considered normal? Or will it be a question of how we all adapt and change to what is now the new normal? We'd love to bring our restaurant back from this, but when, we don't know. There are just too many questions that have yet to find answers.

Dreams, for the most part, are fickle things, evolving as time passes and circumstances change, spending their lives rolling around the perimeter of our minds, giving us a brass ring to reach for, to work towards. The pursuit alone can be enough to fill a lifetime. But when they're finally realized, they have the power to reshape our thinking and sharpen our vision, to the point that nothing will ever seem impossible again.

It was a short run, the dream we built, but man was it intense. Kauai will always be our home now, there is no place that either one of us would rather be, so we'll wait it out and see if maybe the island shows us something new. For now, we've tucked the Garden Island Grille into storage, put away the Aloha Stage, and carefully wrapped up the greatest moment of our lives.

# The End.

Beer flight

Dragon fruit margarita

Sheri runs the bar

Dave working a busy afternoon

Napoleon's dream coat

Aloha Stage at Christmas

Bring on the tuna

Chef Jeric

A look behind the bar

A unique wedding

Dave lights up the stage

Dave and Sheri and the bare-naked linguini